W9-AKP-394

Portrait of Venice

Giandomenico Romanelli

Portrait of Venice

Photography by
Mark E. Smith

Edited by
Cesare M. Cunaccia

RIZZOLI
NEW YORK

First published in the United
States of America in 1997 by
RIZZOLI INTERNATIONAL
PUBLICATIONS, INC.
300 Park Avenue South,
New York, NY 10010

First published in Italy
in 1996 by
Arsenale Editrice srl

ISBN 0-8478-2035-1
LC 97–65575

Translated by Antony Shugaar

Printed by EBS Editoriale Bor-
tolazzi-Stei, Verona

Printed in Italy

Contents

Venice
Its appearance and history

A city unlike others

The city of Venice was not founded in the usual sense of the word: there is no original layout or street grid, no plan that follows a geometric scheme, and no elaborate design based on astral or cosmic influences and themes. In short, there are no surviving signs of a strong intent on the part of the original inhabitants of the city—although there is no question that, in the centuries that have elapsed since Venice was first inhabited, enormous time and energy, and many mental and dialectical acrobatics have been expended in an effort to accredit an acceptable myth of the city's ancient origins.

Apart from those efforts, and equally early—certainly dating from the first literary testimony concerning the city—Venice's uniqueness and distinctive qualities, both of impregnable power and religious significance, engendered a widespread familiarity with a number of specific features of the city. It was the diffuse knowledge of those features that led to an accretion in the mass subconscious, and a profusion of adjectives and sobriquets regarding the city that has not ceased to this day. All this in an effort—most often a vain effort—to explain and illustrate, describe and catalogue the meaning of an inherently Venetian state of being, and to delve into the roots and the reasonings of that condition.

The great problem of transforming this unique city, of bringing it in line with the technology of other cities, arose repeatedly—even obsessively—throughout the course of the nineteenth and twentieth centuries. During these years, the architectural structure and the quality of life in the city as it had been under the *ancien régime* seemed inadequate; improved communications, a solution to the daunting obstacle of Venice's insular state, and an industrially based economy all seemed to be answers to the problems plaguing Venice, which afflicted the city increasingly in the years following its demotion. Venice passed from the status of independent capital to that of a provincial town caught in the meshes of larger institutions or international politics (variously, the Napoleonic empire or the reign of the house of Hapsburg). The tragedy of Venice dragged itself out in a progressive loss of identity, waning hope for the future, a failure to plan, and in the gradual deterioration of the city's physical structure—this last bestowing on the city the physical and moral form that

7

finally made it one of the world capitals of the Romantic movement and, later, of the European decadent movements.

In spite of all this, Venice continued to live and to renew itself; amidst crises and difficulties of all sorts, it experienced periods in which once again the city stood as a model of civilization, and even as a workshop for the creation of the future.

The coexistence of these different and often contradictory spirits creates the present-day complexity of the Venetian condition; the city is the ground upon which lacerations and crises—as well as the incomparable cultural itinerary that Venice represents—continue to sketch out a singular adventure of human civilization. The spaces, the sites, the buildings, houses, and churches; the various elements of proportion and language (in all the many meanings of that word); the interweaving of void and solid, of interior and exterior—all of these forces and features have contributed to creating the city as it is, giving Venice its unique character and continuing, for better or worse, to make it a living city, endlessly shifting and changing form in an ongoing succession of skylines and identities.

This is one of the reasons that any given fragment of Venice can become, in a unique instant, the true face of Venice. An example: a wall in Campiello Angaran contains a remarkable stone tondo from the twelfth century. This tondo depicts a Byzantine emperor holding the terrestrial sphere and a sceptre, and on either side of it hover four carved stone shells of *pietra d'Istria*, like four huge leaves of lettuce forgotten on a now-empty dining table. The tondo is a symbol of the majesty and the listless everyday existence of a great architectural banquet served in the eighteenth century. That supreme majesty and languid daily routine mingle, making the impossible possible, allowing opposites to be reconciled.

A portrait of Venice must foresee the unpredictable. It must also take into account a remarkable form of time, the different way time passes in this city, which here is an intrinsic component of the form things take. According to one interpretation of this, one must move through Venice in strict accordance with the sound of footsteps on stone, or the gentle splash of oars in water; nothing, however, could be less accurate than this idea, nothing more squalid than the use of this imagery in support of the most sordid commercialization of the very soul of Venice.

Carnival festivities, regattas, balls, lavish parties, festivals, liter-

ary awards, historic processions, nostalgic re-enactments—none of this is enough to restore the long-lost dignity of Venetian modesty and charm. Venice, more than ever, must be portrayed chastely, if the city is to reveal what survives of its past and embrace its future. Once again, the form of this city contains all hope for the future, and room for architectural design and planning.

A long and unbroken ribbon stretches from the earliest vestiges of Venetian style—already in spectacular evidence on Torcello—to modern-day Venice, the Venice that is relying on new technologies for its future existence because it appears increasingly certain that preservation is a great tribute to the past, and at the same time the greatest promise for the future survival of Venetian life. The preservation of the city's form represents a victory of the future over nostalgia, a victory of planning over inertia, and the indefinite extension of the unstable equilibrium that has always constituted the political and cultural underpinning of Venetian life.

Island and terra firma

It is quite difficult to avoid the trammels of a double pitfall: on one hand, there is the trap of depicting Venice in terms of the most threadbare literary images, and on the other are the shoals of lost categories, essential to an understanding of the city, which have been tossed out with the commonplaces and clichés. The splendid history of a millennium-old civilization has come down to us through citations and references and in anthologies of masterpieces, and later still, in the survival of moldy revivals and shameless imitations of the past. This history must be written with a clear understanding of the remarkable success of its own mythology, in the terms of the serpentine development of Venetian historiography. It is also necessary to peer into the heart of present-day Venetian life if we are to glimpse the modernity of this collective undertaking. Venice, amidst all its tribulations and contradictions, is still a city of culture, of remarkable ways of life, of incredible experiences that take shape in the *forma urbis*, or physical manifestation of the city—in the various features that have made Venice a vital and functional system.

Architecture, open spaces, structural details, *calli* and *campi*, churches, places of work and of manufacturing, inner courtyards, scattered sculptures, open courtyards, outdoor staircases, mosaics, frescoes, portals—the continuum that is Venice winds in a labyrinthine and ever-changing course throughout the body of the city. Wherever transformations have taken place, there deterioration and renewal have chased one upon the heels of the other. And in that sense, as well, the city may appear—and not only in the present—as a sort of workshop for the preparation of the future, of possible Venices.

Access to Venice nowadays is primarily by one of the two routes that so profoundly marked the structure of the city in the nineteenth century, and again in the twentieth century: the railroad line (inaugurated in 1846) and the highway/causeway (built and opened to traffic in 1932–33). Prior to the opening of the railroad line, one reached the city either from the Adriatic Sea, mooring in the great Bacino di San Marco, directly in the political and ethical heart of Venice, or else on boats of various sizes which set out from any of the many terminals on terra firma, serving to ferry non-Venetians to various points on the northern edge of the city. Even for those arriving from the sea there were intermediate passages, especially during times of epidemics and pestilence: quarantines in lazarets, passage through the checkpoints of the maritime health commission, customs areas, disembarking from large seagoing ships onto smaller lighters. Whatever the original point of departure, and whatever the landing site, until the middle of the nineteenth century all travelers were obliged to abandon dry land at some point, entrusting themselves to a smaller or larger vessel—and such was the case until the railroad bridge was built. And it is here that we find evidence of the most profound shift in status in Venetian history: no longer an island, the city lost a distinctive trait of its Venetian condition. This shift rapidly undermined the occupation and importance of the guilds of the boatmen, longshoremen, transporters, and others. These two modern connectors have, at least partially but in an irreversible manner, reduced the degree to which Venice is different from other cities, limiting this difference to the way in which one gets around, and the way in which goods and cargo of all sorts are transported within this lagoon city.

The two major projects (railroad and highway), built nearly a century apart, were hardly painless: the polemics, disputes, recriminations, and regrets are countless. Even now, many believe that the problem of connections with terra firma is the sole obstacle to the city's economic recovery because hindrances to transport and the costs (in terms of time and money) caused by the intricate division of shipments, and the need for repeated trans-shipping, eliminates the competitive edge of any business located in the city (even in executive, administrative, scientific, cultural, and tourist-driven fields), discouraging investments and economic commitments from businessmen.

Since the building of these two major access paths, the aspects of the city that the traveler meets are, in most cases, a front entrance that still retains considerable originality, but also is plagued with chaos and confusion, and a rear entrance that has become a showcase to which it is not equal. It is necessary, then, to set off along other routes, seeking other destinations in order to construct a more credible and authentic image of this city. Still, no one should hope to stroll through Romanesque or Gothic Venice, or through scenes from canvases by Canaletto; there have been too many renovations, too many successive stratifications, nearly suffocating the city—crowding a reality that is still physical and available to experience.

There are still a number of powerful urban centers that have maintained their importance even though they may have lost their original function. Among these are the area around San Marco, the area around Rialto, the immense military shipbuilding machine of the Arsenale, and the vast structures of the churches built by mendicant orders, along with their adjoining convents. Clearly, the very heart of the system has always been the sheet of water that extends from the San Marco area. Indeed, the little square that is now known as the Piazzetta di San Marco—to be precise, the area enclosed between the Palazzo Ducale and the Libreria di San Marco—was for many years unquestionably the inner port, the wet dock of the system. At once a city hall and a hall of justice, both prison and palace, the Palazzo Ducale (Doge's Palace) has stood as an extraordinary

opposite
*Sketch of Venice in a pilot-book
(detail) by Giovanni Xenodoco,
Museo Correr (thirteenth century).*

manifestation of political power, and of that power's splendor and generosity to the arts. The Basilica di San Marco, originally a ducal chapel (it was not transformed into a cathedral until after the fall of the Republic, under Napoleon), represents, on the other hand, a deep and beloved link of the city to both the Byzantine tradition and its Roman counterpart. Above all, however, the basilica is the fullest and clearest demonstration possible of the rightful apostolic standing of the Church of Venice—a national institution that long proclaimed its substantial independence from the Roman Church.

Structure and image: origins

The earliest known effort to describe in writing the image and character of Venice portrays a landscape and its inhabitants in all the ambiguity of their amphibian nature: they could plow the sea and sail across their fields. This passage was written by Cassiodorus, prefect of the pretorian guard under Theodoric. In a renowned letter (537–38) written to the maritime tribunes of the Venetiae he described in simple terms, but with unquestionable evocative power, the basic outlines of perhaps the most successful and longlived of the many myths that make up—no less than the stone and marble—the history of this city: a poor but fiercely proud people; a community of equals without hierarchies, free of the sources of discord to be found in more-complex societies; self-sustaining; the importance of trade; tireless labor to drag the earth from the grasp of the sea. In short, he described a volatile and unsettled environment, an endless give-and-take between water and land, between the solid and the precarious.

Literary contrivance, then, rapidly covered over the concrete and positive meanings of a series of historical facts: wars and conquests, voyages and discoveries, institutional reforms and coups-d'état, industrial revolution and economic decline, state religions and popular devotion. A continuous and massive cultural project was set up, explaining, interpreting, and justifying the complex process of development of the state, an historical adventure with highlights and dark stains, heroism and great wickedness, great leaps forward and sudden retreats. What survives, immune to misreading or differences of opinion, is the urban structure itself, unique and unrivaled; and

the continuity of an unparalleled artistic culture producing a remarkable wealth ranging from music to literature, from painting to architecture—perhaps no other Western nation can boast such a long and glorious artistic season. This city represents the highest peak and the richest and most varied synthesis of this complex period. Perhaps more unusual is the fact that, on the whole, Venice has survived substantially intact to the present day, and that it therefore provides us with a guided tour of the objects, the symbols, and the words of a narrative that suffers only the occasional gap, and in which the rips and tears were quickly and handily stitched up, as if by a spontaneous healing of the city's tissue.

The earliest known map of Venice shows the size and shape of the city in a substantially final form; we can see the locations of the oldest and most important religious buildings, as well as early indications of the administrative structure. Those churches, sharply marked urban focal points, canals, and embankments, those outlines marking the almost emblematic shape of a fish—all can still be experienced and verified, all appears simultaneously to our senses, following a history that might appear in some cases illusory in a space that might invoke the ambiguous nature of a hallucination. And yet this site is quite well consolidated. Its origins extend much farther back than the cartographic documentation of its existence might lead one to believe—indeed, earlier than the frenzied period of barbarian invasions that led to the wholesale flight of Venetian settlers into the lagoons. The pre-Roman period forms part of the first chapter of a history that, although nebulous and largely obscure, involved a substantial settlement on these sites, in close connection with the large urban centers of Padua and Altino. The effect of the rivers was decisive in the configuration of a shifting, unstable lagoon geography, which oscillated almost as frequently as the cycle of the tides.

The lagoon territory was skirted, or in some cases actually crossed by the major Roman roads. The typically Roman definition of property and function—centuriation, or division into hundreds—extended sharply into the area of what is now the lagoon. This indicates the far smaller size of the lagoon in Roman times, and prompts us to imagine the former, exquisitely agricultural territory, with cultivated fields, farms, roads, and villas.

10

"Maritime Venice" and its territory

A dense network of canals and branches of various rivers allowed freedom of navigation within the littoral strips, allowing easy and direct communications with the hinterland and with the various cities. The lagoon area and its immediately adjoining areas, then, became a true crossroads for both land and maritime communications, and for travel across wetlands and marshes, and along river courses: this was a land of encounters and conflicts, and a staging ground for travel to the East.

In the first few centuries of the Common Era, Milan, Ravenna, and Pavia were each to become capitals, but it was through the Venetian bottleneck, like through the narrow fissure of a clepsydra, or water clock, that the great armies and barbarian hordes slowly made their way to and from the great universal poles of attraction, Rome and Byzantium. Between Ravenna to the south and Aquileia to the north extends a procession of cities with paleo-Venetian, Etruscan, Roman, and Byzantine origins; the ties to Byzantium, through Ravenna, provided the greatest political and institutional influence, deep-rooted and persistent, on the nascent lagoon state. The Venetiae were, taken as a whole, a territory that comprised the coastal area (or "Venetia maritima") and terra firma, or the continental section, meaning the hinterland.

In the meantime—and certainly coming to a head with the geo-climatic crisis of the sixth century—the territory continued to be modeled and transformed. The lagoon extended its area, the termi-

nal sections of several rivers shifted (Adige, Brenta, Bacchiglione, Sile, and Piave), new riverbeds were excavated in the wake of disastrous flooding, a number of littoral strips were sharply defined and staked out, and full-fledged islands formed amongst the mud flats, the shifting sands, and the unstable lands of the lagoon. One of the fundamental points of conflict in the ongoing political and military struggle between Byzantines and Longobards over the course of the seventh century was here, precisely along the Adriatic coastline: trade routes, salt, control over communications with the East, and most importantly, merchandise and goods from the East, endowed these areas with roles and potential profits of enormous importance. The convergence of various peoples and different languages, the necessity of maintaining open diplomatic channels—even during the bloodiest wars—the role of mediator that repeatedly fell to the city of Venice, the close contacts with Byzantine fleets and, in time, Longobard and then Frankish armies—all of these factors worked together to form the personalities, outlooks, vocations, and sensibilities of the free men of that amphibious world that would eventually become Venice. First they gathered around a *magister militum* named by the Byzantine court; in time, he was replaced by a *dux*, then a duke, a ruler who grew increasingly independent but who never entirely cut off ties with Byzantium.

These ties, although they may have limited freedom of movement, were all the same the source of imperial legitimation. The selection of Mark (of direct apostolic descent) as patron saint contributed to a mosaic of beliefs, myth, and politics that was destined

13

Details of the excavation and the mosaic floor (opposite) of the old church of San Lorenzo.

to endure for centuries, and which would endow the national Venetian church with a standing of pre-eminence over the surrounding bishoprics, in time endowing Castello-Olivolo with the patriarchal eminence that was taken from both Grado and Aquileia, and finally ensuring it a remarkable degree of independence even from the throne of St. Peter's in Rome.

Bishops, monks, abbesses

Venice's condition as a border state and, at the same time, a fundamental hinge connecting with the main structure, can be singled out as one of the most meaningful of the remarkable characteristics of Venice. This condition was in-effect and quite solid at the turn of the ninth century when the two small islands at the center of the lagoon of Olivolo and of Rivoaltum-Rialto were selected as the episcopal see and headquarters of the doge-dux.

The fundamental organizational status was that of a dukedom governed by a substantial pact of confederation among numerous townships and other centers scattered over a sizable territory that comprised the littoral areas, the intermediate zone of lagoon and mud flats, and the first expanse of solid land, or terra firma. By the tenth century, the whole area extended from Loreo to the south, near the mouth of the river Po, all the way to Grado. The physical core that provided the focus of the system (that is, the new city that had Castello-Olivolo and Rivoalto-Rialto as its salient points) had already attained considerable solidity and complexity. This city was further consolidated by the growing structure around San Marco—both St. Mark as the patron saint of the entire community, and the actual site of San Marco, meaning the physical site in which St. Mark's body was preserved. This first basilica dedicated to the Patron Saint, Protector of Venice, soon came to represent an exceedingly farsighted investment, in moral, political, and economic terms: this basilica served to tear away religious predominance and authority from the older and more renowned island of Torcello. Above all, however, this focal point managed to draw into its hands—through economic dynamism and political shrewdness, and due to environmental and logistic advantages, as well as sheer functional versatility—offices, powers, leadership, and wealth from all over the duchy.

That duchy, in the space of just a couple of centuries, would appear as if all its independent ambition had been sucked dry by its Venetian neighbor, becoming merely a docile handmaiden to the city's power and dominance.

Other players and forces emerged on the lagoon landscape between the eighth and the ninth centuries; among others of particular power and significance were the various monastic settlements. Controlling immense landholdings, active in the reclamation of land through various cutting-edge technological methods, possessing and preserving a massive cultural heritage, and dynamically deployed throughout the European chessboard, the monks of the various Benedictine families immediately appear as remarkable factors in civilization and urbanization. The monasteries soon proved to be fundamental centers of power in the development of economic and political dynamics in the Venetian duchy. At the edge of the lagoon, on the islands, and along the littoral, as early as the eighth century we find Benedictine monks and nuns at Certosa, Sant'Ilario, and Brondolo. Exceedingly close to Piazza San Marco, at San Zaccaria, stood a Benedictine convent that, from its very foundation, proved to be a wealthy and powerful institution. It housed girls of the ducal family (that is, the family of the doge). Near there, at San Lorenzo, the sister of the doge Orso Partecipazio founded another Benedictine monastery. Its landholdings extended all over the city, and on the mainland as far as Treviso.

In the years that followed, settlements proliferated. Prior to the year 1000, the monastery of San Giorgio Maggiore was founded. In the same general period, the monasteries of San Basso and San Leone on Malamocco and those of San Secondo and Sant'Erasmo on the tiny island of San Secondo were founded, as were San Nicolò al Lido, Sant'Angelo della Polvere, San Giorgio in Alga, and dozens other religious communities, convents, and monasteries, which enjoyed greater or lesser success, but all of which contributed to the remarkable concentration of work, piety, culture, and charity that served to nourish life and civilization in and about Venice. What certainly should not be undervalued was the coexistence in the Venetian world of different currents of influence: the eastern, Byzantine current; the western current of Longobard and Frankish origin; the Roman, classical current; the Po Valley current; and the Northern European current. In the history of art and in the development of

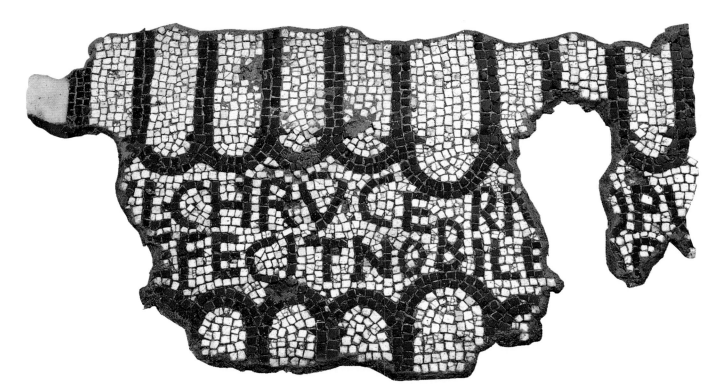

visual styles in particular, these influences were fundamental, and certainly shaped the long season of creativity punctuated by various cultural waves of philo-Byzantine or Westernizing styles, even after the fall of Byzantium in 1453.

City and architecture

As late as the tenth century, the shortage of surviving documentation and even of archeological finds prevents us from shaping much more than a vague delineation of the urban structure of Venice. All the same, very recent excavations and studies have, to some extent, improved upon what we were already able to reconstruct from old literature. This is true, for example, of the discovery of three successive strata of the ancient church of San Lorenzo: the abundance of recycled materials from older sites, both brick and cut-and-hewn stone (present at Altino and all architectural ruins from Roman times) is fully confirmed here; the techniques for packing mud and consolidating it with burnt marsh reeds are also easily discerned here, as is the renowned system of pole-foundations, the establishment of the *zatteroni*, or rafts, made of crisscrossed boards of larchwood, and the installation of hewn-stone foundations followed by undifferentiated piles of crushed stone in the lower layers of the foundations. The Venetian method of building is present in these archaic fragments of an architecture that here is mature and fully developed, having adopted the techniques that accumulated through a thousand separate rivulets and streams, into a civilization, into the forms and styles of the builders of the earliest Venice.

Between the ninth and tenth centuries, growing urbanization gave structure to a substantial portion of what would become the true city of Venice, but it would be naive to suppose that this urban center took the forms and size of the city in later centuries. It was a landscape in which areas of mud flats, broad brackish lakes, canals that continued the watercourses flowing out of the hinterland—all were interspersed with consolidated areas of higher elevation, fortifications (legendary, and not yet fully explained, is a large wall cited in various chronicles, which is said to have extended from Olivolo to Santa Maria del Giglio), and farmlands. This was a continual strip that extended from the eastern extremity of Olivolo, passing through Gemini and then Rivoalto and Luprio, joining up in the west with the area of Canalecto, and giving the nascent city the structure of *sestieri*, or sixths, which was only to take deep root later, from the twelfth century on. The main watercourse (which in time was to become the Grand Canal) had not yet found its definitive bed, although along its embankments, especially in the central area surrounding the sharp curve of Rialto, were the earliest compact nuclei of an organized urban array. Here, and along the axis linking the San Marco waterfront with the nascent area of trade, commerce, and other services at Rialto, we begin to see the first large real-estate holdings that were early enough to mark the structure of the city.

It is not easy to say just what the distinctive features of this structure might have been. By this time many ecclesiastical buildings had already been built; the size and configuration of many channels of communication had already been established; and above all a network of norms and legal formulas reinforced the process of urbanization, reduced misbehavior, enforced hygienic standards, and regulated relationships between the various quarters. But partly because of the fire of 1106, which was so extensive that it destroyed almost a quarter of the city between the area of San Lorenzo–San Zaccaria to the east, and the western extremity of San Nicolò dei Mendicoli, with the Grand Canal as its northern boundary, few noteworthy fragments of the city's architecture have been preserved from such early centuries. We only find durable traces of architecture from a little later, the thirteenth century, when we find typologies that have since become canon. In these typologies the traces of an original architecture are quite faint, long since lost in the elevated diction of more

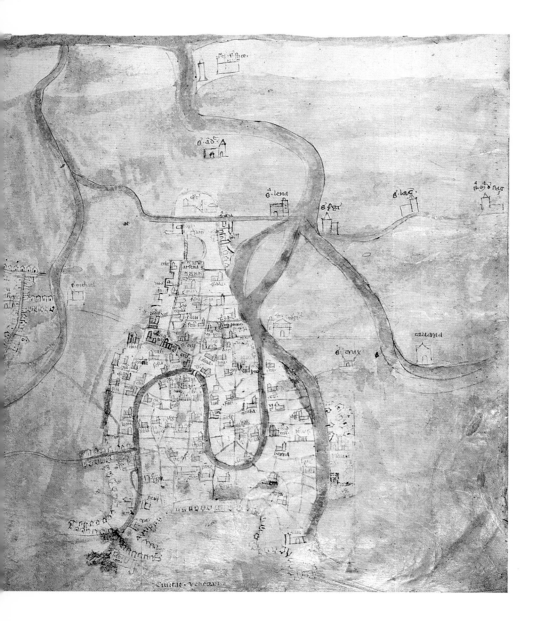

intricate forms and structures based on models that laboriously assembled and blended the requirements of their functions (the *fondaci* with their storehouses, the large grain silos, and the wine cellars . . .) with the no-less rigid requirements of image and decoration. In some cases this also included a desire to preserve archaic typologies that, as such, were credible and ennobling, reliable. This desire may even have embraced the model of the country villa of Roman and late-Roman origins, that had populated first the agrarian territory, and later the lagoon territory, and which impressed a seal of civilization upon the ambiguous world of the mudflats, pools, and canals.

Churches and fire

Matters are even more complex where religious buildings are concerned, although they are better documented by virtue of the surviving edifices themselves, or by substantial portions of them. If around 750 C.E. Castello was elevated to the standing of episcopal see, and if from the ninth century onward there seems to have been an incredible profusion of new religious edifices built around the various centers mentioned previously, it cannot be denied that even earlier, considerable centers existed and prospered in this religious sense, certainly beginning in the seventh century. Dating from the first half

of the eighth century was the first version of San Marco, a structure that, despite fires and periods of neglect and reconstruction, was long identified with the city itself, its identity and culture. Even the style that was impressed upon the basilica when it was reconstructed in the eleventh century presents, to the appraising eye, features that unquestionably reveal its cultural and stylistic roots. San Marco's originality, which was so obstinately pursued in the name of and by virtue of political and ideological eclecticism, allows us to perceive traces of the inspiration of Justinian and of Constantinopolis (the church of the Dodici Apostoli, or Twelve Apostles, is always mentioned in this connection), along with various references to Ravenna, influences of Torcello, the recurrence of the style of the exarchy, and above all, structural and spatial conception of classical, Roman origin. It is also, however, impossible to ignore the links with a certain austere Romanesque style of the same period in what are now France and Germany. This was later to some extent undermined by the continual mantle of mosaics that clad the walls of the building.

16

administrative breakdown into six sections (the *sestieri*), the layout of the perimeter of the inhabited areas, the relationship between land and water and between canals and non-navigable waterways, the location and orientation of the parishes and their churches—all this and more had by this point acquired a form of its own, establishing the layout that for centuries was destined to become the urban icon known as Venice.

The new face of the city

The great fires of the twelfth century were certainly a factor in the instability of the form and image of Venice, and yet at the same time they were a powerful stimulus for the development of the prevailing architectural style; for the long-term adoption of less-flammable building materials; and for the increasingly solid definition of the boundaries between areas that had been thoroughly urbanized and others that were still in conditions of transition from the natural, free-range environment. It is thus that Venice arrived at the age of the earliest cartographic documents mentioned previously. It is surprising to discover the early date (1346) at which a zenithal map (drawn to show correct directions from the center) was produced, far earlier than any perspectival view, and earlier even than symbolical and allegorical depictions. One reason for this may be found in the necessity of nautical cartography, and the absence of any hills or other high points in the terrain may have discouraged efforts to draw an overhead map. In any case, this and other maps are a major point of reference in our efforts to reconstruct the ancient city. The

As we prepare to lay out, to the extent possible, a credible portrait of this city, the weight of such a prehistory is an ineluctable consideration; for centuries this has been the spinal cord, the foundation of the urban aggregation of Venice. On the other hand, this prehistory is composed of unsettling fragments, otherwise undecipherable, of objects that surface as archeological finds from within the continuum of the physical structure of the city. In some cases these finds are only chance stones, tiny jewels set in the slime; in other cases they are absolute masterpieces, glittering with the perfection of a classical marble. The face of Venice is as much a composition of these lesser presences as it is an assemblage of the larger and more spectacular monuments such as San Marco, the Frari, the Redentore,

17

preceding pages, from left
Detail of the eleventh-century plan
of Venice drawn by Fra' Paolino
Minorita around 1346, Biblioteca
Nazionale Marciana.

Imaginary reconstruction of Venice in
the high Middle Ages in a watercolor
from the codex of Tommaso
Diplovataccio.

Mosaic of the transfiguration of the
body of St. Mark, in the vault over the
portal of Sant'Alipio in the Basilica di
San Marco (thirteenth century).

below
Aerial view of Torcello.

or the Palazzo Ducale. For this reason, as well as for its charm and its romantic state of neglect, for the contrast between the exquisite gold of the mosaics and the muddy poverty of the mudflats, the earliest image of Venice can perhaps be seen in Torcello.

A small, poor Venice is what we find at the outset—hardworking, living hand-to-mouth. Everything that is needed to support life here must be brought in from elsewhere. Wood and stone come from the forests on distant mountainsides, from quarries often located overseas, or from those manmade quarries into which ancient cities had declined. Metals, tools, raw materials, wood, fabrics, wine, oil, spices are imported—only fishing ensures day-to-day subsistence. It was not until after the year 1000 that these goods began to fill the warehouses of the merchants, the market squares, the ships, and the carts. And with those goods, there was a proliferation of craftsmen and their workshops: carpenters, stonecutters, kilns for potters, tanning yards, furnaces for glassmakers, shops for the cleaning and dyeing of cloth, spinning and weaving shops, yards for the construction of boats both small and large, and the *squeri* where techniques were developed and solutions were refined for a new and unique form of navigation.

On small expanses of water, above the plants and flowers of the mudflats, amidst the aquatic birds, in the streams and canals that, in the growing city that rose ever higher, still separated islet from islet, mud from mud, mooring spots, foundations, it was necessary that whoever was traveling by boat should be able to row standing up, peering ahead in order to avoid obstacles, keep a safe distance from other boats, navigate safely through the labyrinth of the shallows, properly and safely balance their cargo, and make the best use of the shallow water with the least effort. This was because people, animals, and goods were by and large transported by water—immediately recognized as a great resource, an unrivaled natural defense against enemies and a channel of communication, linkage, unification. It is surprising to note how today many of these characteristics can still be detected in spite of the diffuse modernity, beyond the deforming filter of an invasive monoculture of tourism, and beyond the very commercialization of the image of the city.

Fondaci and palazzi

Reasonably clear traces still survive of the major *fondaci* (storehouses) of the twelfth and thirteenth centuries. The celebrated Palazzo dei

Vittore Carpaccio, the arrival of the English ambassadors in the court of the King of Brittany (detail), in the series of Saint Ursula, Gallerie dell'Accademia (c. 1495).

Pesaro, later deeded to the Turkish nation and in time renowned as the Fondaco dei Turchi, still shows the most throroughly consolidated and the most monumental of the medieval structural typologies—the typology of the family residence, that was also a "trading company" of the first order as well as an exceedingly powerful political party. This typology is detectable behind the mechanical symmetry and the rigid forms of a nineteenth-century restoration (a restoration that nowadays appears to us as devastating, but which clearly shows the state of knowledge and the tools of the trade at its dawn) behind the ancient layout of a house with storehouses, a cloistered courtyard, and sheer sides reminiscent of the fortified villae of ancient Roman civilization. Based on this structure, we can identify a variety of variations: the splendid ruins of Ca' da Mosto, the houses of the Donà, the houses of the Dandolo and the Farsetti, of the Corner Loredan, the houses of the Falier ai Santi Apostoli, the Zane, and the Barziza, and the list could go on at considerable length.

Ranked below the great palazzi are various structures whose recurring features were the large ground-floor porticoes, the loggias on the upper stories, often extending the entire width of the facade, and sometimes there was a third floor, which might be smaller, with fewer windows. The outer walls might well show a complex structure of terra-cotta work, but it was increasingly common to find reworked stone taken from other structures and reused for decorative purposes, partial sheathings in marble of various colors and patterns, odd fragments used in rose-windows and all sorts of compositions. Arches showed—and still show—exceedingly intricate work influenced by late antiquity and the Byzantine era, with such motifs as reeds, fretwork, and flourishes; then came a Romanesque style, with racemes, geometric patterns, dadoes, and other features. Even the capitals—when they were not taken from Roman or exarchal buildings (and adapted for use in such structures as well heads or partitions or screens)—were becoming increasingly refined, progressing from the rough, squared-off cubes of the Carolingian variety to a type with more distinctive features, and inevitably well finished and elegant. Arches with high uprights, marble sheathing, encrustations, and paterae (Byzantine madonnas with open arms or allegorical, even profane animals and monsters)—all these features helped give the city an Eastern flavor that was only to be abandoned with the dawn of the Gothic style. While the great palazzi of the Grand

Canal that date from this phase tended to cluster around Rialto on either side of the channel, it is only in the older, earlier-settled areas that have not changed substantially over the centuries that we find less high-flown traces of this urban development: in San Cassiano, Santa Margherita, Corte del Milion near San Giovanni Crisostomo, and San Pantalon.

Gothic Venice

Beginning with the end of the thirteenth century the architecture of Venice continued to develop in a progressive evolution. There has

top
Photograph of the Fontego dei Turchi prior to the nineteenth-century restoration.

right
Large arch with Veneto-Byzantine motifs in the Corte Seconda del Milion near San Giovanni Crisostomo.

left
*Patera in Greek marble
(thirteenth century).*

below
*Veneto-Byzantine well head with
cruciform reliefs and geometric
decoration, Museo Correr.*

opposite
*Pope Alexander III gives a ring to
the doge, BMC, Museo Correr.*

been considerable emphasis on the nature of this transformation. Was it a gradual modification, occurring through adaptations and updatings of features of thirteenth-century architecture that were, all things considered, more ornamental than structural—or did Venetian architecture change its basic nature in radical terms? There are supporting arguments for both positions. On one hand, we can point out the continuity of structures upon which were overlaid stylistic adjustments and variations, usually consciously, finally resulting in a new stylistic language. On the other hand, one could argue for the complete Westernization of Venetian architecture due to the arrival of Gothic—even though in religious buildings characteristics were introduced that were not only different from those of the "classical" Gothic style (French or English) but also showed from the outset a great stylistic independence, indicating a radical break with Venetian tradition, in part through the lively efforts of popularization undertaken by the mendicant orders.

Whatever one's opinion may be on the matter, the period of Gothic architecture was one of the most spectacular times in Venetian architectural history. Civil and religious architecture, the improvement of living conditions, the creation of a versatile and original architectural language, the intentional creation of an urban setting with specific and well-defined characteristics—these aspects and others suggest that the appearance of Gothic Venice is the appearance that has won the greatest approval and did the most to encourage the unification of typologies, proportions, and technological solutions that were to become canonical in later years. It was not accidental that the *palazzo pubblico*, or city hall, the residence of the doge, and the hall of justice were all combined and unified in a single structure—the Palazzo Ducale—which represents the quintessential aspect of a style that is wholly and exclusively Venetian. (In a rather unsuccessful stylistic touch, the Basilica di San Marco, as well, was crowned with a flamboyant Gothic pediment, over the Byzantine-Romanesque base structures.) Even Gothic civil architecture unquestionably shows the signs of previous structures and styles: the *palazzi-fondaco* to which we have referred, that is, the large houses with a cloister-style courtyard, and huge full-length halls opening on the facade with large *polifore*, or multi-section windows. This sort of structure must be the starting point for an understanding of the

Gothic architecture of most palazzi and houses in Venice. What is lost however is the prevalently symmetrical layout of these structures (and we see this difference in conception in the facades, as well), while the cloisters become porticoes that can be reached both from the land entrance and from the water entrance, and exterior marble stairways link the courtyard to the upper floor. In brief, there is a break with the habit of closure of the structural block, and there is an increase in the number of floors in each building. What remains is a layout that calls for the full-length hall (*salone passante*) with smaller rooms alongside it, along with multi-section windows (*polifore*) along the front, and that distinctive stretch whereby the facade (where possible on the Grand Canal or else on an opening, a *campo*, of considerable size) appears to carry on a discourse of its own, separate from the fairly close layout of the structural block behind it. The front of the palazzo aims primarily to appear as a significant section of the urban system, to fit into a context, interacting with and gaining prestige from that relationship. It is this trait that gives many of the structural curtain walls of the city the personality of both a continuous fabric and a theatrical backdrop: consider Campo San Polo or Santa Maria Formosa, Campo Sant'Angelo and Campo Santo Stefano; also long stretches of the Grand Canal at Ca' Foscari or at the Maddalena, at San Cassiano, at San Moisè. These fragments of the city are only the best known and the most monumental sections of a structural characteristic found everywhere: at Castello or along the Fondamente di Cannaregio, behind Campo San Polo or at Santa Maria Mater Domini. . . .

The mendicant orders

Dominicans and Franciscans settled quite early in Venice, but the enormous basilicas that tower like immense ships over the sea of roofs of Venice are the result of renovations and expansions that went on for decades and decades. These structures had profound effects on the overall development of the city: the northern and the western boundaries of Venice were shaped by a factor favoring consolidation and development, specifically in the presence of the Dominicans and Franciscans. Settling upon land set aside by exceedingly powerful

alegrica amor incontra a nuis lo doxe con le braçe auerte e
disse ben uegna lo signor de tuto el mar. e tolse uno anello
poro elqual el dona a nuis lo doxe digandoi. Sicome ello
sposa la dona cossi uoio che tu sposi el mar i signisicaçion
che tu sie signor de tuto el mar. e dito questo nuis lo papa
baxo lo anello e nuis lo doxe lo gita in mar. Et alora con
orde nuis lo papa a tuti li doxa che ogno anno i lo di dela

sensa el doxe dauesse andar a sposar el mar. ¶ Estando el
fio delo imperator i pinçon houno ora el se dia a nuis lo pa
pa eta nuis lo doxe cheloli uoleua dir algune parole che se
ruisse se bonet. e la nuis lo papa e nuis lo doxe fo cô lo fio
delo imperator. elqual i disse quando el ue piacesse bassar
in gala fe io andarnue uolentiera da mia parte nuis lo impe
rator a tratar pace. e in caxo dela pace no se complisse no
ue prometo i liança de tornar i pinçon. E de questo fo con
tento nuis lo papa e lo doxe. E cossi el fio delo imperator
separti et ande in pina da so pare elqual aue granda ale
greça quando el uete so fio. e de proxente el prega insisie
lo imperator che el amuisse li suo barem che lo li uoleua dir
ar de parole e nuis lo imperator fexe uegnir tuti li suo ba
ron. e cô gran reuerencia prega nuis lo imperator che

noble families (Tiepolo and Badoer, respectively), the monks immediately began to build new buildings and to transform existing buildings, to provide locations for the indispensable features of their pastoral activities: church, convent, and hospice. At first, these were chapels and tiny houses; before long, however, there was a growth in size that corresponded to a parallel growth in importance—political and economic, as well as pastoral and cultural—of the mendicant orders. Enormous construction yards thrived, with consequent shifts in population according to the work of craftsmen, the use of materials, the deployment of resources; the various quarters of the city were shaped around the workshops and ateliers, the marble yards, the kilns for making bricks and roof tiles, the woodyards, and the kilns of the glassmakers. The results of this enormous collective labor were remarkable in relation to the size of Venice: churches such as the Frari, Santi Giovanni e Paolo of the Dominicans and Franciscans, the church of the Servites, long lost, at Cannaregio, the church of the Agostiniani at Santo Stefano, the church of the Lateranensi canons at the Carità, the church of the Umiliati at the Madonna dell'Orto— all marked in a strong manner the structure and image of enormous sections of the city, and even determined the overall physiognomy, as was the case with the larger basilicas.

The experience of the Gothic city was long-lasting. Even today the traces of that period appear as the most continuous and coherent of all the styles, partly because Gothic construction yards occupied the city for so long. The richness of that architectural style also forced historians to define a number of phases. The first, uncertain breaks in the continuity of the indigenous architecture of the thirteenth century (often described as Veneto-Byzantine), undermined a number of lexical and semantic strongpoints—beginning precisely from the roundhead arch on high uprights that constituted an immediately identifiable feature. Developments followed of even greater complexity and daring, including the interplay of marble, rose windows, multilobed fretwork, slender and elegant columns, polychrome decorations, hanging loggias, and corner windows. The Gothic arch went through the various versions of inflected, extroflected, lobed, and composite, in architectural uses of growing complexity and originality; Palazzo Ducale was a constant point of reference.

More than the religious architecture, the civic Gothic of the city of Venice was one of the most elevated contributions by Venetian culture to the artistic languages of the West, even though that Gothic remained a unique experiment, unrepeatable and unexportable. Indeed, the few revivals that are documented, almost exclusively in the cities on the Venetian terra firma, are veritable quotations, when they are not actually stillborn efforts or vernacular imitations of the greater structures to which they refer.

left
*Lauro Padovano (?), Polyptych of
St. Vincent Ferrer, detail of the
predella with the miracles of the saint,
church of the Santi Giovanni e Paolo,
(c. 1500).*

below
*Tavoletta dei Mureri, Museo Correr
(fifteenth century).*

Pope Alexander III meets Frederick Barbarossa, Museo Correr.

for Venice, both for its architectural culture and the founding principles of the city's urban design.

Around the turn of the sixteenth century (and even at the end of the sixteenth century, though in less spectacular terms) the encounter between tradition and modernity was manifested in some of the most remarkable and dramatic architecture in the history of Venice. The new developments from central Italy and Lombardy made their way to Venice. Bold and daring, the new styles showed remarkably lovely structural and decorative aspects, considering the intentional reference to the grandeur and dignity of the classical world. Pastiches hovering between the archeological and the provocative appeared in the earliest work of a singular individual, the Veronese architect and painter Falconetto (who would, as municipal architect in Padua, introduce an influential "modern" classicism). But already in art or in the decorations of funeral monuments or tombs the marks of Gothic were interweaving with a rediscovery of candelabra and grotesques, of Roman and archaic references, with vases, capitals, and pilaster strips, with portals and triumphal arches that once again underscored a yearning for the classical grandeur of the Eternal City, which now appeared on the horizon with its invigorating message, clear and intact despite the centuries of abandonment. And yet the architectural culture of Venetian Gothic conserved all its certainties, its plasticity, the endless articulations of a flexible, reliable instrument in which the vocabulary referred, without the slightest incoherence, to a world of values—civil messages, religious universes, and earthly celebrations. This is why, without shame or concern, the Venetians could build, in two evocative sites (the land entrance of the Arsenale and the great entrance to Palazzo Ducale) the city's two representative monuments, symbols of a period of transitional cultural developments.

Bartolomeo Bon, a master builder who was trained in the Gothic workshops and building yards, would experience directly the contradictions of the transitional situation. He designed the last great Gothic constructions at Palazzo Ducale, and he also encountered the lust for power and modernity that the two wealthiest patrons of the Venetian aristocracy, the brothers Marco and Andrea Cornaro, meant to set forth as a declaration of rank and political ambition. The result was the beginnings of a palazzo on the Grand Canal near

The "modern" city

The last exploits of Gothic architecture are found well within the fifteenth century, when subsequent architectural languages had already been established in the lagoon. Palazzo Pisani Moretta, Palazzo Cavalli, Palazzo Giustinian, Palazzo Contarini Fasan, Palazzo van Axel, and the enormous Palazzo dei Foscari were built around the middle of the quattrocento, as late as the 1480s or the 1490s, and even in the sixteenth century. But it would not be correct to say that this late Gothic was a vestige of medieval Venice that would now be expected to coexist with a modern city. Indeed, modernity has always been a problematic and contradictory concept

San Samuele. Just as it rose from its foundations with the sketchiest beginnings of the revolutionary ground floor, the palazzo was sold to the duke of Milan Francesco Sforza (hence the name with which the street became famous, Ca' del Duca). This palazzo was to remain a fragment: Bon never agreed to deliver the plans for its completion to the new owner, whose economic and political mishaps contributed to put an end to the project around the middle of the century. At about the same time, two men who proved in time to be the real stars of Venice's humanistic and Renaissance period arrived in the city: Pietro Lombardo with his workshop of architect-stonecutters, and Mauro Codussi.

Codussi appears to have been profoundly interested in issues of the layout of buildings and structural solutions of civil and religious architecture; he was well aware of the teachings of Leon Battista Alberti, and had seen his work. Pietro Lombardo, head of the Lombardo family, was far more interested in matters of architectural language and ornament. He took from Venetian tradition a number of ideas of decoration, ornament, and matters of perspective.

Pietro Lombardo and his atelier

The paths followed by Codussi and Lombardo were not identical, though they certainly worked in parallel, and often designed separate parts of the same buildings.

Pietro debuted with the remarkable architectural essays that constitute the great tombs that various doges erected in the churches of Venice. Triumphal arches and cenotaphs, tombs and captioned panels, niches for sculpture, and celebratory compositions extending across entire walls were Pietro's repertoire. Possibly beginning with the church of San Giobbe, Pietro worked on the exquisite exterior *campiello* of the Scuola di San Giovanni Evangelista, and then the bas-reliefs and false architecture of the lower bands of the Scuola di San Marco. His masterpiece, though, was the church of Santa Maria dei Miracoli, with its exquisite polychrome marble, geometric patterns, and sculptures. The underlying architectural grid extends across two stacked orders, the first with a flat trabeation and the second with round arches (there are notable solecisms: the most spectacular is in the rather unsightly basket arch on the front, which extends over a greater width, but maintains the same height as the others). The pilaster strips of the two orders punctuate the entire structure, but the rhythm is hobbled by adaptations required by the irregularity of the plan; the rectangular bays between the pilasters are made of light-colored marble, but every panel features decorations and designs executed in polychrome marble and porphyry. In this way, compactness and structural solidity fall second to the decorative appearance of the whole, which from its very beginnings was considered one of the most sumptuous and splendid buildings ever built.

The silhouette of the church of the Miracoli is that of an unarticulated box covered by a wooden barrel vault with an irregular silhouette, and faced in lead sheets; emerging on the eastern end is an apse surmounted by cupola. The interior is as lavishly decorated as the exterior, and the apsidal area is disproportionately elevated, accentuating the overall vertical effect. Perhaps the most original feature in the whole array is on the side overlooking the canal, where a series of brackets in the shape of Ionic capitals almost seems to hold up the building, raising it out of the water.

It is odd that while he could design a building of great quality, laying it out with new elements and truly remarkable ideas (stacked orders, for example, or the bracket-capitals mentioned above), Pietro would also undercut his own innovative work with excessive decorative choices, which were also often poorly coordinated. This attention to the illustrative aspect of his work, this yield to the temptation of pomp and decor—all was a function of the powerfully ideological and evocative aspect of such architecture. The reference to San Marco and the ancient Venetian tradition became the binding element for a sophisticated cultural operation. It is undeniable that Pietro's workshop was a crucible of experimentation and research: archeological taste, references and borrowings, sculptural virtuosity—this made Pietro Lombardo a personality of the first order in the history of Venetian architecture.

The method visible in the Miracoli was extended to civil architecture by Pietro and his fellow workers and followers. Palazzi and houses featuring the stylistic tropes of the Lombardo family were widespread in different contexts and at every level: from the palazzo of the Dario family overlooking the Grand Canal all the way down to the tiny houses of confraternities and hospices. By this point—although maintaining the tradition of the Gothic stonecutters and master builders—the new, elegant visual language, so useful for production in series and thus so versatile, represented a desire for the new without betraying links with the past.

above
*Inscriptions on the Lombardesque
facade of Ca' Dario overlooking the
Grand Canal (c. 1480–90).*

opposite
*Tullio Lombardo, Funerary monument
of the Doge Andrea Vendramin, church
of the Santi Giovanni e Paolo
(c. 1500).*

Mauro Codussi

Codussi was aware of local architecture (the tripartite fronts of churches and their curvilinear coronations were common practice in Venice as well as in Dalmatia, and the same was true of the dome roof and the central plan in churches) but he interpreted those aspects in an elevated context, selecting subtle and evocative grace notes, and clear-eyed philosophical and theological concepts, to the point that there have been theories of a neo-Byzantine period that stretched from the end of the quattrocento to the first three decades of the sixteenth century. From the little church of San Michele in Isola to San Giovanni Crisostomo, by way of the campanile of San Pietro di Castello and the great church of Santa Maria Formosa, Codussi refined his visual language with dynamic solutions highlighted by the use of elements in Istrian stone, slender columns and pillars, and by simple mathematical proportions in which the central

plan played a defining role in establishing the logic of the organic structures. In civil architecture Codussi was a tireless inventor, and built surprising new forms. Palazzo Zorzi, Palazzo Lando Corner Spinelli, and above all, Palazzo Loredan Vendramin Calergi are all the outstanding products of the most up-to-date experimentation in the Venetian idiom, at an advanced point of equilibrium between the Florentine and Central Italian culture and the interpretation of the genius loci. Even in these structures we sense the influence of Gothic architecture; the plan may even make vaguely ironic reference to Gothic characteristics. The large T-shaped hall of Palazzo Loredan carries forward the weight of a long tradition, but the elegance of the material and forms, the monumental dignity of the various elements (note the powerful, yet elegant cornice) allow it to be compared in quality and clarity to the great altarpieces of Giovanni Bellini. Codussi was also responsible for developing an architecture, neither religious nor private, of remarkable dignity and impor-

tance—that of the headquarters of the leading *scuole* (literally, schools) of Venice. These were devotional or professional confraternities who played a major role in the social and charitable life of the city. The Scuola di San Marco, like the Scuola di San Giovanni Evangelista—and in another setting, like Bergamasco Bon's Torre dell'Orologio, the clock tower in Piazza San Marco—defines clearly the settings and potential of this new architecture, which is fully and originally Venetian. The traditional orders of Vitruvian architecture made their entrance: round arches became the distinctive feature of these structures, along with barrel vaults and gore vaults, hemispheric cupolas, square-face pilaster strips, rosettes, caissons, ribbings, twin-light oculi. The Piazza San Marco itself, at the time of the refabrication of the entire northern side, was to be—beginning with the Torre dell'Orologio—defined by a grid in the idiom of Codussi. This, as well as the kaleidoscopic repertory of the Lombardo family, was the true language of the Venetian architecture of humanism and

the early Renaissance. Including the monumental constructions of Giorgio Spavento and Tullio Lombardo (especially the great basilica of San Salvador) and of Antonio Abbondi Scarpagnino, this was the core of that dissipated heritage described by Puppi, to be supplanted by the Romanist triumph of Jacopo Sansovino beginning in 1530.

opposite
Antonio Rizzo and Mauro Codussi,
Palazzo Ducale, detail of the fifteenth-
century front overlooking the water.

above
Lazzaro Bastiani, The offering of the
relic of the True Cross to the brothers of
the Scuola di San Giovanni Evangelista,
Gallerie dell'Accademia (c. 1494).

Jacopo de' Barbari, Detail of a woodcut bird's-eye view of the city of Venice, Museo Correr (1500).

The myth of Venice in the early sixteenth century

It was with the arrival of Sansovino in the city, presumably in 1529, that certain factors condensed to establish a profound turning point in the development of the architectural culture of Venice. Political difficulty and military defeats (the League of Cambrai and the defeat of Agnadello in particular) radically altered the self-confidence of much of the ruling class. Suddenly they were no longer unbeatable. The territory of the state was partly occupied by enemy armies, and the Venetians no longer showed the characteristics of aggressive and impetuous entrepreneurial venture that had so characterized their early economic success. Threatened on the Mediterranean by the Turks, and uncertain even of the central role of that sea following the voyage of Christopher Columbus, the Venetians needed a sense of security and an affirmation of their raison-d'etre. These years of the early sixteenth century were a time of retrenching, of profound cultural revision; in these years the cultural and artistic vocation established its authority, allowing the Venetian spirit to live in the imaginary space of a remarkable literary myth. It was the city itself that created this myth and allowed it to survive. It was, however, the task of a handful of architects and theoreticians to transform that myth into palazzi, houses, streets, churches, monuments, public buildings, and villas.

With the fall of Rome and its sack and plunder by Imperial troops in 1527, artists from the Eternal City brought to Venice the talent and style of Rome, the influence of the Caesars, and the artistic language of the papal court. Jacopo Sansovino, Sebastiano Serlio, Giulio Romano, Michele Sanmicheli, and an entire genera-tion of painters and decorators headed north across the river Po in search of patrons, clients, princes, and thrones. Already in contact with members of such major Venetian dynasties as the Grimani and the Cornaro, Jacopo Sansovino arrived in Venice, never again to leave. The mark that he was to leave on the Venetian cityscape was the root of a radical cultural shift.

Chronologically and conceptually balanced between the early Renaissance of the Lombardo family and Codussi, and that of the Roman style and Sansovino lies the true masterpiece of Venetian car-tography—the woodcut bird's-eye view of the city, dated 1500, by Jacopo de' Barbari. From this fundamental source of knowledge and

understanding, we clearly see the structure of the city: two centuries of Gothic construction and the first two decades of renewed architecture have, by 1500, filled every square and saturated every open space, especially in the more central areas of the city. Even the northern and western borders (where for two centuries medicants and preachers had been at work), although not yet fully urbanized, were constituent parts of the urban system, with only a few remaining wooden huts or sheds. The Venice depicted by de' Barbari is clearly a complex organism, vital, dynamic. It is busy challenging and interacting with the terra firma that can be glimpsed in the distance; it is integrated with the system of lagoons and littorals, but above all, it stands out in that it is wholly man-made, an artificial and astonishing work of art.

Jacopo Sansovino: the Roman style

The work of Jacopo Sansovino represented Rome. His sources were classical Rome as well as the Rome of the Popes—the Rome of Bramante and Raphael, Peruzzi and the Sangallo family on one hand, and on the other, the Rome that had already begun to reveal its hidden archeological treasures, over whose marble relics architects and scholars were raptly bent, over whose ruins the most daring and reckless itineraries of fantasy and imagination were being pursued.

Venice was originally intended as one step on the great journey into France for the young Sansovino; instead Venice was to become his workplace for the next fifty years. Sansovino introduced philology, respect for the grammar and syntax of orders, grandeur of conception, a substantial detachment from existing structures and styles, and hence a freedom to maneuver that had been hitherto unthinkable. The requirements of mythology (both literary and rhetorical) soon became the Magna Charta of the work of Sansovino, who made Venetian architecture, in the words of Manfredo Tafuri, "the art of the state." At first he was involved in a series of projects that may fairly be described as light revisions, but in 1529 he began working on a major structural project in the Basilica di San Marco. He then set to work to complete construction on the north face of the Piazza San Marco, and thereafter went on to build an entire series of public and private buildings: Palazzo Dolfin and Palazzo Cornaro,

the Ospedale della Ca' di Dio, the churches of San Francesco della Vigna, San Geminiano, San Zulian and the complete and monumental redefinition of the entire complex of St. Mark's—Piazza San Marco, the Piazzetta, the Riva del Molo and the various buildings overlooking it—as well as the immense and unfinished structure of the Misericordia, houses, monuments, and sculptures. Palazzi and churches played a major role in Sansovino's Venetian work. The outsized Palazzo dei Cornaro—which came in the wake of a project for the Grimani family that never made it off the drawing board—represents the most impressive and daring presentation that Sansovino could have made of his work. The entire facade is organized in accordance with that of the Teatro Massimo in Palermo, while the ground plan, with its enormous square courtyard, was likewise laid out with the correct succession of orders and endowed with massive halls. Overlooking the Grand Canal from an unusual vestibule structure preceded by a grand stairway and a horizontal portico, the home of the Cornaro family was intended to amaze the onlooker, and to set forth the proportions of a new and unparalleled grandeur. The material employed was primarily Istrian stone, which was used on the ground floor with disconcerting effects, giving a sense of new and massive rusticated brutality rather than the elegance and polish of preceding styles. This, the size of the corbels in the large windows, the vast, continual series of windows on the upper floor—all of this proclaimed the grandeur of a family, no less than the dignity of the city, successor to ancient Rome and favorite offspring of Byzantium.

Piazza San Marco

Sansovino's construction in the area around St. Mark's fully defined the ideological significance of the area. Overcoming the resistance of the forces of tradition, the Procuratori and the group of senators that had coalesced around Vettor Grimani, Pietro Bembo, and in general, the Romanist faction entrusted Sansovino with the job of building the Libreria di San Marco, facing Palazzo Ducale just beyond the Piazzetta. Then, on the front overlooking the Molo (mole) and the Bacino (basin), he built the new Zecca (mint). Then followed the loggetta at the foot of the Campanile di San Marco (St. Mark's

belltower) and the renovation of the Scala dei Giganti, or stairway of the giants in Palazzo Ducale, with its two huge statues of Mars and Neptune. At the far end of the Piazza, facing the basilica, Sansovino built the new church of San Geminiano. Considering the lesser renovations done within the basilica, the completion of the Procuratie to the north, the reconstruction of the Molo with the construction of the Ponte di Pescaria, and the work done on the important artery of Calle Larga San Marco, we can see how Sansovino was able to implement the great plans of his patrons. According to their wishes he created a Piazza and surrounding areas that were absolutely unprecedented, grandiose, modern yet clearly ancient in style, functional, with a fine view, theatrical and astonishing to any visitor, while at the same time capable of serving as an architectural backdrop for the epiphany of Venetian power.

In order to provide such a renovation of the Piazza, Sansovino was obliged to shift the alignment of the Procuratie to the south, and to isolate the Campanile, which was, however, recycled as the pinion of the perspectival system that was thus created. He also cleared away the shops and stalls seen in the depiction by de' Barbari, which overlook the Molo where one day the Libreria and the

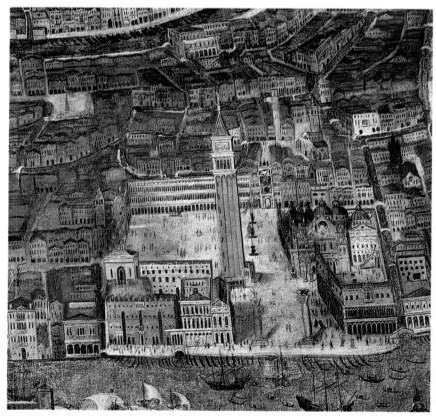

opposite, top
*Roberto Roberti, The Piazza San
Marco looking toward the church of
San Giminiano, Bassano del Grappa,
Museo Civico (eighteenth century).*

opposite, bottom
*G. B. Arzenti, Detail of a view of
Venice, Museo Correr (late sixteenth
century/early seventeenth century).*

*Michele Sanmicheli, Forte di
Sant'Andrea, facade overlooking
the lagoon (1543).*

Zecca would stand. This aligned the entire area for purposes more theatrical than functional: the Piazza—vital, disorderly, organic—made way for a piece of theatrical, perspectival machinery.

Sansovino proved to be gentler in this respect in his renovation of the Fabbriche di Rialto complex on the far side of the bridge—still made of wood—that linked the two banks of the Grand Canal, including the area of the Fondaco dei Tedeschi, recently burnt and rebuilt, the marketplace, finance, and crafts quarters, and the major technical and financial magistracies.

Sanmicheli and Palladio

While Sansovino was radically re-creating the appearance of the city at its most sensitive points, the Veronese architect Michele Sanmicheli was attempting to restore coherence to the military defense of the Venetian territory, so badly humiliated by the recent defeats. As he had done in Verona, Peschiera, and Dalmatia, Sanmicheli employed a spare, eloquent architectural language. The Forte di Sant'Andrea facing the harbor mouth at Lido is a handsome example of this type of architecture adapted to the horizontal landscape of the lagoon, like a powerful, silent guard dog hunkered down to protect the priceless treasures of the family.

Still, when he faced the challenge of civil architecture, Sanmichele unleashed a range of solutions and ideas that almost prompted jealousy in his friend Sansovino. He was agile in the Palazzo Cornaro di San Polo, taking direct inspiration from the architectural drawings published by Serlio, while in the palazzo built for the Grimani family on the Grand Canal at San Luca, Sanmicheli constructed a machine, as it were, of unusual monumental scope and sweep. This palazzo was gigantic on the ground floor and in the massive arches of the upper floors, emphatic and yet carefully finished in every single detail, and illusionistic in the false perspective that masks the irregularities in the ground level. There was no real effort to emphasize the contradiction between the front and the body of the building, which seem summoned to lead two different existences: the everyday routine of the bedrooms and kitchens, service areas, alcoves, and dressing rooms oppose, on the Grand Canal, the triumphal arches of a powerful and aristocratic family with boundless ambitions—cyclop-

ean architecture suited to a humanity of heroes and giants, demigods and demiurges.

Just a few years later, another major figure appeared in the lagoon area: Andrea Palladio. Unlike Sansovino and Sanmicheli, Palladio did not come from the building yard of St. Peter's under the supervision of Bramante. For Palladio Rome was a destination long dreamed of and the subject of a thorough and scientific study (to the point that one recognizes in the reliefs on Roman monuments the origin of the function and appearance of the architectural systems developed by Palladio). He really studied somewhere between Vicenza and Padua, amidst antiquarian influences, literary infatuations in the wake of his mentor—the aristocratic man of letters of Vicenza, Gian Giorgio Trissino—and observation of the work done by Falconetto for Alvise Cornaro.

Palladio was in time summoned to shape considerable sections of the Venetian territory, and placed remarkable seals upon the land with his villas and gardens, inventing an astounding new architectural language, exceedingly personal, that brought together the sacred and the profane, Christian church and pagan temple, country home and city palazzo, irony and gravity. The degree of ambiguity, and hence of poetry, in Palladio's inventions nonetheless made him a suspicious character, and politically difficult to employ. His work remained outside Venice proper for some time, and it was only after the death of Sansovino that Palladio would truly work in the lagoon area, but only in religious architecture.

Beginning in 1576 Palladio worked on the design of the church of the Redentore, and then went on to design the church and complex of the Zitelle, followed by the church and part of the convent of San Giorgio Maggiore. He also designed the front of Sansovino's church of San Francesco della Vigna and the convent complex of the Carità, with its famed cloister and its version of the house of the Romans.

The effects of Palladio's work can still be seen today, and they are remarkable from every point of view. His was an architectural language that was at once archeological and new, in which the fronts of classical temples were used to cover architecture of unusual monumental scale and clean, essential geometry. By this time the authority of Andrea Palladio's theories had supplanted even the ancient mastery of Vitruvius and the modern word of Alberti. Palladio's was a

form of design that worked on the territorial scale, extending across the great spaces of landscape, whether those were the plains or the hilly slopes of the countryside around Treviso, or the edges of the lagoon or the secondary branches of the river Po. In any case, Palladio clearly showed his intolerance for schemes and constrictions, aiming at a scale of intervention that sought a dialogue with the setting, with the landscape, in an attempt to manage the landscape and the territory.

Likewise, in the major churches, and especially in his masterpiece the Redentore, Palladio's subtly balanced structure is functionally complete unto itself, perfectly calibrated to its site and to the various points of view that bring it to life, making it clearly understandable and profoundly meaningful, a fragment of the city capable of conferring dignity and logic to an entire city profile. Palladio was completing an investigative journey beginning in the uncertainties and doubts of the early Renaissance, but his arrival at his final objective was hardly a sure thing. In the metaphoric battle between a native Renaissance style and the architectural language of the Roman school—with the momentary triumph of the latter over the former—the sun was setting on a period, a method, and a way of living that were rooted in bygone centuries.

Continuity and renewal

The work of Sansovino and Palladio, and to a certain extent Sanmicheli, caused a breakdown in continuity of the Venetian architectural language. The Veneto-Byzantine tradition, the Romanesque and Gothic cultures, and even the period of the early Renaissance had developed semantic systems that were linked through distinct terms and morphology. Even the new classical developments of the mid-sixteenth century were slowly reabsorbed into the fabric of continuity, but initially they constituted a problem that affected ideological and political progress. Otherwise, there would be no way of explaining the tenacious opposition to Palladio's work in both civil and public architecture, the alignments opposing or favoring the renovation of the entire southern side of Piazza San Marco in a project that would replace the thirteenth-century architecture with a Mannerist interpretation of the Libreria by Sansovino.

In the face of such powerful and spectacular creations (the churches by Palladio and, on the other hand, those by Sansovino; palazzi by Sansovino and Sanmicheli; the fortifications of Sant'Andrea by Sanmicheli; funerary monuments in numerous city churches; the San Marco complex), the lesser, residential architecture continued to weave its web over the entire territory of the city. It consolidated the marginal areas, urbanized the peripheral strips, gave a solid, recognizable form to that minuscule portion that still survived of the

precarious huts and rough banks. This spread expelled from the center of town the small boatyards, tanneries, fullers' shops, and the many dangerous or polluting industries, which were replaced by entire residential quarters, unified and organic complexes meant for the less wealthy classes still capable of maintaining a dignified lifestyle. The Scuole invariably pursued these objectives. In this context the houses of the Scuola di San Rocco are exemplary in quality in terms of both structure and urban planning. Certain still-detectable sixteenth-century residential complexes offer a documentation of the character of these areas: the organization of the buildings and building lots in residential modules extending horizontally or vertically; rational layout and functional systemization; a canny use of materials, and above all, a brilliant use of the Istrian stone that linked projects of this sort to higher Venetian architecture, thus ensuring the quality and durability of the structures.

"Not one city, but many separate cities joined together"

Many of the distinctive features of sixteenth-century urban Venice become clear in a renowned chapter of the first great description and guide to the city, published in 1581 by Francesco Sansovino, the son of Jacopo.

So many and such wonderful buildings, then [the author has just finished a list of the most important palazzi in Venice, both ancient and modern], with others adjoining of greater or lesser importance, form a broad and magnificent city. This city, if considered carefully, proves to be not one city, but many separate cities joined together. Wherefor if one considers the layout of the entire area, seen in plan, without bridges, one can see that it is all broken up into many large *castella* and cities, surrounded by canals, over which one passes from one bank to the other by bridges, most of which are made of stone, some of wood, joining them both together. And thus it appears that these are many different cities joined into a single great city, due to the many workshops scattered throughout the entire territory of this city. Because each quarter has not just one, but many churches, a square with wells, ovens, wine cellars, the guilds of the tailors, fruit vendors, spice merchants and chemists, school teachers, carpenters, cobblers, and finally every other thing that may be useful to human purpose, in great abundance. So that, if one leaves a single quarter and enters into another, one would say without a doubt that one had left one city and entered another, with enormous convenience and satisfaction of all the inhabitants, and the astonishment of all outsiders.

The wealth of the patrician homes corresponded to an equally lavish distribution of services and public facilities as well as a presence of trade, craftsmen, and professional organizations distributed throughout the city. The network of canals continued to be the most convenient and affordable system of communication and transportation of goods; indeed all contracts for the construction of buildings contained special clauses or specified agreements with *battellieri* and *burchieri*, who would transport the building materials to the site and remove the waste material to dumps, and for the handling and treatment of all sorts of goods and supplies, including raw materials and finished products needed in the building yards. The beds of the canals were constantly dredged to prevent clogging and silting that might have interfered with the passage of boats and greatly compromised the healthfulness of the area. Then, as now, the constant tidal flow constituted the most effective way of eliminating the liquid and solid refuse produced in Venice, both organic and industrial (waste from dry cleaning and dyeing, tanning, glass works, and other workshops of all sorts).

Many streets were paved, and in some cases even illuminated at night; bridges made of stone, according to the writings of Sansovino, were replacing the old wooden bridges almost everywhere; decoration of the public facades of private buildings was closely controlled, and no work could be done that had not been approved by the appropriate offices, whose clerks and surveyors were constantly out and about, checking and measuring in response to requests for permits or reports of illegal construction or renovation.

Returning to the heart of the city, without ignoring the polycentric essence of Venice, we would reiterate that without question the Bacino di San Marco (St. Mark's basin), which attained a consolidated form by the end of the sixteenth century, imparts meaning to the entire urban system. The disastrous fire in Palazzo Ducale in 1576 and the long drawn-out process of rebuilding cast light on a number of new issues: the decision to rebuild "in style" (i.e., to rebuild the palace in the same Gothic style that had characterized it before the fire) reinforces the massive ideological significance of the consolidated image of the area as a whole (the suggestion by Andrea Palladio of a classical-style reconstruction was rejected). The operation also provided an opportunity for a new layout of the palace's decorative structure in accordance with specific iconographic programs, creating lavish official spaces adorned with remarkable series of paintings designed to exalt important historical moments of the Venetian Republic.

By the end of the century, then, the area around Piazza San Marco had been condensed by the recurrent and interlinked architecture made of Istrian stone, from which emerged the perspectival framework of the Loggetta, the Zecca, the Libreria, and so forth. It is remarkable to note the apparent search for solutions that were then immediately contradicted and built to live out an impossible coexistence. It is hard to say whether all of this forms part of some open polemic on Sansovino's part toward the increasingly solid and focused Venetian continuity. And yet, the emblematic case of the way in which the metope of the frieze at the corner of the Libreria is bent around that corner, was transformed by the Venetian circle of art and culture (and specifically by Pietro Bembo) into a sort of public exercise for experts in architecture and archeology from all over Europe. These experts would discuss specific and general themes pertaining to the discipline, not so much with a view to accommodation or mediation, but rather in the spirit of examining a method and a philology that still met resistance from the traditional pragmatism of the Venetians.

The invasion of baroque culture

A new development of enormous importance was to be introduced into the St. Mark's area over the course of the seventeenth century, resulting in a fundamental shift in equilibrium. This development was the construction of the majestic basilica of the Madonna della Salute, built by public referendum in the wake of the murderous outbreak of the plague in 1630. In effect, the Salute introduced a visual fulcrum of exceptional efficacy, forming with the complex of the Punta della Dogana, which lies before the Salute along the water like the prow of a ship, a central point of reference that had previously been lacking. The very silhouette of the basilica, with its strict central plan surmounted by a hemispherical cupola set on unusual marble scrolls, emphasizes the perspectival function of the building and endows it with a truly monumental scale.

The baroque period, with respect to the magnificence of the cinquecento, may have witnessed a slight decline in Venetian supremacy in the area of painting, but in the field of architecture it saw a phase of great research and creativity. Besides the church of the Salute, Baldassarre Longhena built civil and religious buildings, both private and public, and revolutionary in terms of the idiom (among them we should note the gigantic Palazzo Pesaro and the small but brilliant church of the Ospedaletto). Moreover, Longhena (who, like the Sardi family, was one of qualified architects of the Venetian baroque) showed a special aptitude for projects that involved a major section of the city surrounding the chief building or structure. This was the case with the area around San Giorgio dei Greci, the area around the Salute/Somasque convent-Punta della Dogana, Palazzo Pesaro and Palazzo Bon (later Palazzo Rezzonico), the convents, and so on. This aptitude certainly did not originate with the

41

great Baldassarre Longhena: what we might call a theatrical attention (for an exquisitely urban stage setting) can be seen in the fifteenth-century open courtyard of San Giovanni Evangelista; in the renovation of the area around Castelforte at the time of the construction of the Scuola di San Rocco; or in Santi Giovanni e Paolo with the complex of the Scuola di San Marco/church-monument of Colleoni; or Santo Stefano with the creation of the open/closed space before the Palazzo dei Pisani—and in a hundred other projects and areas.

Complexity and ambiguity

Sites throughout the city present similar features in which the ambiguity between the closed and the open, the inside and the outside, the public and the private, comes to be one of the possible methods for dealing with the organization of urban space. This approach shows that it is possible to alter the very manifestations of life in order to take part more intimately in the polycentric, labyrinthine, wholly artificial form and the life of the city.

Already, in the words of those who observed the form of the city and wandered through its narrow *calli* and *campi*, Venice was charged with an unsettling allure, enigmatic and contradictory. To others it appeared to be exemplary, admirable for its architectural daring, unique in terms of material and aesthetic richness. Foreign observers spied with respect and curiosity upon the endless labor required to perpetuate the coexistence of water and land, elements in a continuous battle for an unthinkable victory; the fury of the sea and the

treachery of the tides were no more dangerous than the silting of the rivers, the spread of the mudflats, and the general pollution. This endless dialectic led to the creation and destruction of political alliances and cultural attitudes, built up fortunes and triggered disasters, brought life, and in its wake, brought death. Titanic undertakings moved rivers and created canals, reclaimed valleys and plains, or caused the creation of swamps and the spread of malaria: the most advanced scientific and technological knowledge (at times applied in the most obtuse and rigid ways, shrouded by the guise of official rhetoric) and the most go-ahead pragmatism (often not equal to the challenges of the projects) had the city and the lagoon as a test lab.

In the sixteenth and seventeenth centuries the city expanded only slightly: there was a complete embankment of the northern shore and the western terminus, and the island of the Giudecca experienced a definitive accommodation as a suburban area, with villas and parks. The villas in terra firma on the other hand were one of the great areas of expansion and investment of Venetian capital: the great enterprise of the villa began early in the sixteenth century, and was destined to continue for more than three centuries. The Venetian countryside toward Padua and Treviso, around Verona and Vicenza, and even in the treacherous lands between the rivers of the Polesine, and in the territory of Friuli, all witnessed a continual welter of hundreds and hundreds of new villas: houses, palazzi, *rustici*, *barchesse*, gardens, vegetable patches, parks, *piscine*, fish ponds, mazes, odeons, loggias. Everything contributed to the expansion of the cultural dominance of Venice, imprinting the seal of a civilization that was impossible to copy. The very architecture generated an exclusive

visual language, much emulated throughout the world, to respond to this new frontier of the villa. Columns, capitals, pronaoses and tympanums, rustic and aristocratic orders, vast thermal windows, cupolas, vaults, pinnacles and turrets appeared across the countryside. The powerful classes of Venice and the Veneto (both patrician and civic) devoted themselves to the cause with passion, determination, and genius (and huge investments). The Venetian countryside became a paragon to be imitated in England, Russia, Poland, and the United States, particularly in Virginia and Georgia.

Over the course of the seventeenth century, there was a significant shift in direction in Venice: unlike the trend in preceding centuries, renovations of buildings were more common than new constructions. The city at this point was so densely built up and so thoroughly populated that there was no room for new houses or palazzi. Nonetheless, demographic progress showed signs of decline: following the plague of 1630 the population fell to less than 100,000, and then fairly rapidly climbed back to 140,000, but did not return to previous levels.

Scenic and theatrical Venice: between standard and invention

The availability of money and the desire for a new architectural and artistic language soon led to a great fervor and thriving of architects and painters, stucco artists and decorators, carpenters and upholsterers. This baroque, excessive Venice, theatrical, illusory, and celebratory, is the Venice that still triumphs in churches and palazzi in the remarkable trompe l'oeils, the untruthful architecture, and the historical and mythological scenes of Parnassus and Olympus.

This aspect of Venetian civilization still reaches out and entrances visitors to many palazzi; it envelops in luxuriant marble groves the facades of countless churches, barely restraining lions and monsters imprisoned in the most artificial of architecture. The facades of churches such as San Moisè, the Ospedaletto, the Scalzi, of buildings such as Palazzo Pesaro or Palazzo Rezzonico, offer an appearance of civic architecture that is at once admirable and recklessly daring. But even in examples of a more relaxed imagination, the battle between rule and license does not deteriorate into open warfare. The demands of rationality require respect for the proportions of construction, no less than the specific characteristics of materials and the demands of functionality—and such demands were to become prevalent from the mid-eighteenth century on. Elegance and invention, variation and virtuosity together guided the hands of the architects and the

the condition of being a traveler, a voyager, would almost become synonymous with being Venetian in the eighteenth century. Most of the artists in fact were travelers, tracing a dense network of routes, moves, and exiles across the entire continent: Casanova, Canaletto, Giovanni Battista Piranesi, Rosalba Carriera, Giovanni Battista Tiepolo, Count Francesco Algarotti, Sebastiano Ricci, Giovanni Antonio Pellegrini, Bernardo Bellotto, and Carlo Goldoni, all the way down to Giacomo Quarenghi and Antonio Canova. All of them worked to build, around the world, the greatest and grandest Venice that had ever been conceived or desired, without physical boundaries, a place without location or time—virtual, perfect, detested, fundamental, at once abject and virtuous.

The eighteenth century: the final triumph

The eighteenth-century city made famous by Romantic and decadent literature (the literature of the *ridotti* and the boudoirs, the theaters and the *casini*, of sinful convents and crowded bedchambers—as well as the literature of the terrible prisons and ruthless tribunals, of espionage and betrayal), which owes a great deal to travelers and adventurers, does not amount to a full portrait of one of the richest and most varied periods in the history of Venice any more than a mere listing of artists, some great and some less so, who worked in this lagoon city, would complete that portrait. If we pursue different paths we shall also glimpse the face of a hard-working miserable metropolis, in rags, barely getting by: the city of the poor, with a subsistence economy, crowds of beggars and invalids, thieves and thugs, strolling merchants and misfits of all sorts. In the hidden and often infernal folds of the great urban machine, everyone found a precarious little niche of one kind or another, furiously defending their own desperate state. There are still relics and memories of this Venice: where the flow of tourism has remained in the distance, where the locations are least appetizing for speculators and developers, where the apartments cannot be used as second homes. Here and there a *calle* or the occasional *corte* even today are surprising scenes of misery and suffering, serving as rudimentary yet effective time machines, taking us back to years of widespread poverty and suffering, to periods when epidemics carried off tens of thousands of citizens in a

brushes and chisels of artists and sculptors, as if in an exquisite musical theme, to give face and figure to modern Venice.

The monsters of the Ospedaletto and the exotic references in the facade of San Moisè were now abandoned in favor of the angels, scrolls, and fluttering garments of entire celestial courts hovering on the fronts of such limpid and luminous churches as San Stae, the Pietà, and the Gesuati. Pronounced chiaroscuro and contrasts were supplanted by the transparency of the heavens of Tiepolo, the lightness of Arcadian countrysides, and gold and white clouds upon which perched Apollonian deities and pink, sensual putti.

The dawn of the eighteenth century marked the beginning of the last great season of Venetian culture, a final and remarkable adventure experienced by this city on an international backdrop. This is the most renowned image of Venice, ineradicable from the collective memory and imagination because of a remarkable campaign of self-promotion, and self-redesign of the city's appearance, an effort that enjoyed the assistance of a remarkable band of popularizers, the Venetian view painters. But it was a group of artists, writers, and adventurers that served as the most effective and popular means of publicity and celebration of the myth of a liberal and libertine Venice, a sensual and mysterious city, learned and cynical and unscrupulous. These individuals were to export, in their own personalities, bodies of knowledge, and personal inspiration, throughout Europe, the Russias, and the Americas the culture and flavor of Venice. In time

few days or weeks. Not only the terrible plagues from the fourteenth to the eighteenth century, but cholera and typhus well into the twentieth century, struck a populace that was rendered vulnerable by cold and hunger, poorly housed in hovels without running water or hygienic facilities (the new aqueduct reached Venice only in 1882; until then, public or private cisterns for rainwater were almost the only water supply), exposed to all dangers and all exploitation. The nineteenth-century reports on sanitary conditions in Venice are often appalling cross-sections of a situation of total social, human, and cultural breakdown, in a criminally irresponsible setting of decay and neglect, the collapse of housing and of the city as a whole. Awareness of this condition led to the first collective efforts to restore and rebuild both the buildings and the social structure; these efforts, almost always prompted by philanthropic spirits, led to a new season for Venice, a season of light and shadow, amidst dangers and serious problems, a season that leads almost directly to the present day.

The end of the Republic, then, came about in a convergence of causes: the total incompetence of government and aristocracy and the impossibility of reforming a fossilized, decrepit institutional system; external military and political pressures, first and foremost of which was the expansionism of France under Napoleon; the widespread restiveness of the Venetian territories, intolerant of the demands of the capital; and aspirations to democracy and self-determination largely inspired by the spreading enlightenment culture and encouraged by foreigners, secret sects, and Freemasons. At the end of the eighteenth century, then, Venice experienced a period of vast cultural mobilization, and it became once again one of the most advanced and forward-looking centers of the great European debate, both in terms of art and architectural theory and in terms of thought concerning the city as an organism; and concerning every aspect of theater (from architecture to acoustics, from historicist citations to decor, from theater's educational role to the social functions of theatrical performances). Other questions and matters of

Jan Grevembroch, Venetian trades: the pile-driver, Museo Correr (eighteenth century).

much maligned early nineteenth century; for the most part, these periods produced first-rate work.

Between the artistic culture of eighteenth-century rococo (a school that in European painting has its Titan in Giambattista Tiepolo) and the world of the neoclassical (whose leading light and champion was, in Venice and in Europe, Antonio Canova) lies, in architectural terms, the very productive and successful period that gave an elegant and diffuse appearance to churches, palazzi, and urban sites of all kinds. Giorgio Massari was the most successful and active architect in Venice in this period: churches such as the Pietà, the Fava, the Gesuati; Palazzo Grassi or the modern wing of Palazzo Rezzonico all attest to his skill. Other architects such as Domenico Rossi and Andrea Tirali moved further in the direction of a recovery of the classicist style inspired by Palladio. Tirali went so far as to work in Palazzo Manfrin at Cannaregio with a rational and anti-decorative architecture showing an absolute rigor and almost an ideological value.

Neoclassical epilogue

In the end, it was the architect and theorist Tomaso Temanza who originated the symbol/object of the new architectural culture: this was the little church of the Maddalena, with its circular plan, classical pronaos, and cupola. Taking inspiration from the Pantheon and Palladio's projects for central-plan churches, as well as from the little temple of Villa Barbaro at Maser, the Maddalena, which received a chilly reception for its excessively "secular" treatment of a religious theme, immediately became an exceedingly important point of reference for successive generations of architects. In terms of urban planning, the church of the Maddalena was a brilliant and unusually free introduction of a new building into the delicate structure of the Cannaregio quarter. And in time it was a pupil of Temanza, Giannantonio Selva, who received the conceptual bequest of the master, thrusting himself into the spotlight of public patronage and private clients with his design and construction, in 1792, of the Teatro La Fenice, a theater that can be considered a manifesto of the new neoclassical culture in the city of Venice. The presence of Tiepolo and of the great late-baroque and rococo pictorial decoration—prior to

great interest were also present in the world of Venice and the Veneto: there were debates on guilds and corporations, on the organization of the arts and protectionism in economics, on free trade, agriculture, and the theory of the physiocrats. And yet all this debate took place as if with a sobering sense of a last act, of the final moments in which splendor and misery mingled in a new awareness of the fundamental uselessness of planning for the future. It would be inappropriate and ridiculous to generalize; and yet the existential pain of a civilization without hope, this sort of final discomfort is evident in a number of different indications (even without falling back on overused observations concerning the recurring flights from Venice and death in exile of the leading characters of the late eighteenth century).

The appearance of the city still owes a great deal to the second half of the eighteenth century, just as it owes a great deal to the

being ousted in favor of the new neoclassical style, which was to become dominant beginning in the 1780s—had stimulated a remarkably successful artistic season. The series of paintings in churches and *scuole*, decorating the ceilings and walls of palazzi and villas, in ballrooms and bedrooms, great staircases and little dressing rooms— all became the settings for scenes and characters sprung from the imagination of the decorators themselves. We can still see a demonstration of this in Ca' Rezzonico and in Palazzo Sandi, Palazzo Labia, in the Pietà, at the Gesuati, and in the Scuola dei Carmini. The activity of the decorators of the neoclassical, post-Tiepolo period was certainly no less intense: dozens of palazzi, homes of the petit bourgeoisie, rectories, public houses, and offices were updated to reflect the new styles. Amphitrites and Muses, the three Graces and the dance of the Hours, Ariadnes and Theseuses, Orpheuses and Icaruses, Achilles, Chiron, Hercules at the ford, Andromache and Hector, Neptune, the Parcae, or Fates: all of them are depicted on light-colored walls, surrounded by neo-cinquecento grotesques, laid out between geometric friezes. These figurines have constructed the environment and established the form of the literary imagination of multiple generations of Venetians between the eighteenth and nine-

teenth centuries, Venetians living between the final glories of Venice and the astonishing exploits of Napoleon, the return to the Mittel-European order of the Hapsburgs and the revolutionary gusts of 1848. These figures populated the ceilings of theaters, mute witnesses to the performances of Haydn in music halls, observers of meetings of great scholars in the universities and in honored academic institutes, lively features of bathrooms and boudoirs, and cordial backdrops in the modern coffee shops of the time.

Even the official sites of power made widespread use of neoclassical architects and decorators in order to give form to new democratic principles or to design with splendor and elegance the liturgical apparatus of royal epiphanies: first the "new men" of the Jacobin interval, then Bonaparte's imperial affirmations, and finally the inflexible and efficient universe of the late Empire and the Biedermeier style, under the two-headed Hapsburg eagle.

opposite
*Giandomenico Tiepolo, Pulcinella
at rest, Ca' Rezzonico
(late eighteenth century).*

A battle against history

The greatest effort made in this phase of the history of Venice consisted of proposing new interpretations of this urban organism, interpretations that might allow us to forget, or at least play down the memory of the centuries of history of the Venetian Republic, and that simultaneously might suggest a rewriting of the urban signs that would allow us to designate and sustain the new functions assigned to the city and to its various component parts: public gardens, museums and academies, free port, hospitals, and cemeteries. While all of this would mean, in other cities, undertaking operations of demolition and reconstruction, in Venice it meant a considerable effort to reinterpret existing structures, to adapt historical buildings to new uses, and to renovate entire complexes founded in the distant past. If we then link up all of this with the consequences of the ecclesiastical policy of suppressing religious orders and confiscating their possessions, combining various parishes together, one can clearly understand that within the course of just a few years a major portion of the city was involved either directly or indirectly in the renovation process. Demolitions and readaptations involved churches, convents, monasteries, devotional schools, venerable hospices, and charitable institutions. A new city thus arose, with perfectly identifiable characters and forms: the public gardens in the Sestiere di Castello (where the Venice Biennale is now held); the unified general cemetery on the islands of San Cristoforo and San Michele; the Accademia di Belle Arti with its galleries in the former convent and Scuola della Carità; the new headquarters of the Patriarch alongside the Basilica di San Marco; the Portofranco, or free port, and the goods warehouses at San Giorgio Maggiore; a huge parade ground (only partially completed) at the Giudecca; a renovation of entire sections of the Arsenale. There were also new canals between the Arsenale and the harbor mouth for sizable ships; massive fortifications overlooking both the sea and the mainland; barracks, civil and military hospitals, and so forth.

But it was above all Piazza San Marco that experienced—both in terms of architectural structure and in terms of the uses of its buildings—the most profound renovations. At first (in the few months under Jacobin-inspired democracy) it was merely a matter of eliminating the memories of the oligarchic government run by the Venetian aristocracy with ingenuous allegorical and educational decorations, or with the erection of a Tree of Liberty in the center of the piazza; later, however, things became much more concrete and permanent. Napoleon and his court, above all, wished to create in the piazza a seat of power that might sweep away the old signs of Venetian political institutions. At issue, then, was the matter of couching the imperial court in spaces and volumes that would unequivocally mark the presence of a palace, and to do so precisely on the site where previously a delicate system of weights and counterweights previously had been erected to exalt and conceal, celebrate and dominate the figure of the doge as the center of power in Venice.

One entire side of the piazza was demolished and rebuilt in new forms, resulting in the loss of the sixteenth-century church of San Geminiano; the Libreria Sansoviniana and the Zecca, or mint, were transformed into royal apartments; in the new wing a grand staircase of honor, and a large hall for ceremonies were built. It was not until a few years later, well into the time of the Hapsburgs, that the Palazzo Patriarcale, or patriarch's palace, was built amidst all these new constructions. Both the structures of the royal complex and the Palazzo Patriarcale, as well as the older buildings of the two Procuratie were refitted to accommodate the neoclassical style; a crowd of painters, sculptors, stucco artists, frescoers, trompe-l'oeil artists, cabinetmakers, upholsterers, workers of bronze, carpenters, and marble workers undertook to transcribe the entire system into a neoclassical mode. Toward the Bacino di San Marco, in the wake of the demolition of the ancient Gothic sheds of the Granai (grain siloes), a small, enchanting garden was laid out, complete with neoclassical pavilions and belvederes. This garden can be seen today, although it has fallen into general neglect, victim to the squalor of sales operations bound up with the tourist trade.

Between Kingdoms and Empires

The end of Venetian history as a separate concept, despite all efforts to maintain and even to restore some part of the forms and institutions of the ancien régime, caused a sharp break in an institutional continuum that had been in place for many centuries. The aristocracy lost

its privileges, social organization was disturbed, and the economy was revolutionized. Above all, an independent and sovereign state was once and for all canceled from the world stage, and became the property of larger, composite political institutions: in succession, the Austrian Empire, Napoleon's Kingdom of Italy, the Lombard-Venetian Kingdom, again the Hapsburg Empire, and the Kingdom of Italy under the House of Savoy. The single glorious interruption was that of the revolutionary Repubblica of 1848–49, when before the eyes of all Europe the populace of Venice succeeded in redeeming itself from the ignominious blot that had stained the escutcheon of the aristocratic ancien régime in 1797. The revolutionary forces withstood a terrible siege and repeated Austrian attacks—nonetheless, Venice fell back under the military rule of the field marshall and count Johann Joseph Radetzky. Changes in regime and institutional overthrow were certainly traumatic events, but they also tended to introduce dynamic factors into the city as an organic complex. In terms of architectural form and lifestyle, these succeeded in establishing profound and irreversible changes.

Removed, as previously discussed, from its traditional condition of insularity and forced to become similar to a nineteenth-century mainland city, it was necessary for Venice to seek out and determine the styles and forms of its own participation in modernity. It did so with difficulty, paid a number of exceedingly high prices for the process, and lived some deep-rooted contradictions; in the end, though, Venice set out with admirable courage on its new path. At the end of the nineteenth century Venice appeared on the interna-

tional scene with a brand-new role, with credible projects for social and economic redemption, notable results in administrative terms, and a significant and renewed capacity for intelligent planning and design. What had happened in a century of transition and intense work and planning, and what exactly did the leap into the contemporary world promise?

These are questions to which there may be no answer, unless by examining the visible form of the present-day city we can identify the signs with which modernity has marked crucial passages, and guess at the city's future.

The urban planning of the nineteenth century

The neoclassical city was equipped with public services and structures, and was organized in accordance with the principles that informed urban planning at the turn of the nineteenth century: widened streets, straight avenues, broad views, reclamation projects. The Commissione all'Ornato took it upon itself to oversee, issue

directives, promote, and encourage, as well as to attempt to reconcile the interests of public decorum and esthetics with the profit incentive. The government of the neoclassical city undertook great public works, and through a policy of major projects it rationalized and rendered functional the organism that is now Venice: markets, schools, libraries, museums, hospitals, cemeteries, public parks, and so forth. At the same time, there was a simplification of the relation of cause and effect: because the maintenance of some waterways proved to be prohibitively expensive, while an absence of maintenance resulted in menaces to hygiene and public health, the decision was made to fill them in or cover them over; because the preservation of palazzi required immense expenditure on the part of their owners, the owners often chose to demolish them and sell the building materials; because residence on lagoon islands proved to be troublesome even for religious communities, it was decided to abandon the various islands. Similarly, venerable churches and convents were closed down, and there was a systematic dismantling of precious architectural and decorative complexes, monuments, and abbeys; collections were dispersed, libraries destroyed, celebrated art galleries put on the auction block, and valuable archives broken up. In cases where the logic of an economy in profound crisis is not enough to explain the disgraceful happenings of this period, we should simply add to the mix the greed and cynicism of unscrupulous merchants and old proprietors, or the nouveaux riches and reckless heirs.

Even today these lacerations appear all too clearly to those who know where to look: the gaping void replacing the immense church of the Servi, the empty spaces of the former churches of Sant'Angelo, Santa Maria Nova, Sant'Agostino, Sant'Antonio di Castello, Santa Lucia, Celestia, Santa Ternita, the Vergini, San Paterniano, San Severo, and so forth. It would be impossible to list the palazzi, houses, and entire blocks of buildings that have been lost, in many cases replaced by other, more recent constructions. Practically all of the grid of buildings that extends from Piazza San Marco to the area of San Luca across the Bacino Orseolo, and from there as far as San Bartolomeo, is the result of demolition and reconstruction done in the nineteenth and twentieth centuries; a great deal of the quarter that extends from Piazza San Marco to Santa Maria del Giglio has witnessed radical reconstructions. Entire thoroughfares for foot traffic within the body of the city were the result of public works completed in the nineteenth century. The very first was built by covering over the important Rio di Sant'Anna and creating the broad avenue that was first named Strada Eugenia and has since been renamed Via Garibaldi. The main thoroughfares crossing the city and the ring-routes connecting important points in the city embody principles of urban planning typical of the nineteenth century, amidst reduction of distances, reclamation, decoration, urban business, and real estate speculation. The civic aspects of the work being done under Napoleon were gradually disappearing: by the middle of the century almost the only surviving factors were the incentives of profit and speculation; philanthropical works replaced the commitment of the public sector in ensuring adequate conditions and quality of life.

The neoclassical architectural language of the nineteenth century

*Nineteenth-century iron bridge
in the Ghetto Nuovo.*

had bred its strongholds in the city of Venice, and Giannantonio Selva was its most prestigious and versatile craftsman: after the Teatro La Fenice, he designed for the municipality both the Giardini di Castello and the city cemetery at San Cristoforo (though both of these were more demolitions than actual constructions) and he built the church of the Nome di Gesù and also lent a hand on the huge public works involved in opening the Accademia di Belle Arti and its galleries (though they were completed by his pupil Francesco Lazzari). A great deal of work was also done by the architect Lorenzo Santi (who completed the so-called Ala Napoleonica, the Palazzo Patriarcale, and the Coffee House in the Giardinetto Reale), while a good number of other architects, many of them pupils of Selva, were involved in renovations, new constructions, reconstructions, and adaptations. In the middle of the century, however, while maintenance was going forward on a considerable number of important urban structures, new architectural methods were being introduced, and the use of new materials and modern technology became more common. A great many bridges were rebuilt according to a new prototype, and a number of others were made of iron and cast iron. The neoclassical style was losing its dominant position, and was progressively replaced by a neo-Gothic style as a *stile nazionale*.

Historicism, planning, modernity

Giambattista Meduna was the great champion of the age of historicism, as far as the architecture and urban planning of Venice is concerned. Active, versatile, authoritative, and pragmatic, Meduna contributed to urbanistic decisions in the years following Italian Unification (following 1866, with the entry of Venice and the Venetian region into the Kingdom of Italy). He helped create the modern appearance of the nineteenth-century city of Venice, and implemented the policy of major restorations that allowed him to work on the Ca' d'Oro, Palazzo Cavalli, Palazzo Giovanelli, and even the Basilica di San Marco. Meduna was caught up in violent international debates concerning his casual approach to restoration (Ruskin attacked him directly) but without a doubt he also created a number of architectural masterpieces (the stairway and interiors of Palazzo Giovanelli, the commercial building at the Ponte del Lovo, the reconstruction and the interior decoration of the Teatro La Fenice). With Meduna—inventor, as it were, of the Venetian neo-Gothic style—historicist eclecticism established itself, directing a spotlight on the question of restoration and the reuse of antique or ancient architecture.

In the 1880s and 1890s (after a commission dominated by Meduna and established at the same time as the annexation of Venice to the Kingdom of Italy had established the general lines of the future urbanistic policy of Venice) the need for a first Piano Regolatore (zoning plan) and a plan for the reclamation of the city became central. The plan was passed, amidst national and international debate, in 1891.

With increasing frequency, Venetian matters were becoming testing grounds for a more generalized condition of urban culture and its various contradictions. The case of Venice was emblematic of a more general condition in the Western world: the grandeur and decadence of a civilization, conservation or transformation, philology or interpretation, historicism or modernity. Nor should we forget that this paradigmatic condition was engendering a new and parallel literary and mythological reality that was double-faced—at once late-Romantic and decadent, involving death and mystery, and also questing for power and neo-Imperial self-affirmation. The city of Venice as it appears today was built for the most part during the troubled decades of the late-nineteenth century and in the no-less-important decades of the early twentieth century. Activities of these years included the Piano Regolatore; an attempt to industrialize; a policy of affordable, working-class residences that led to the construction of entire quarters in various sections of the city; the rediscovery of the island of Lido (as a tourist and beach resort but also simply as a residential neighborhood); the progressive expansion and growth in importance of the railroad station and the commercial port, with a consequential expansion of the infrastructures linked to them. These were years dense with cultural activity and experimentation: the Venice Biennale was created, the Museo d'Arte Moderna

Marcello Nizzoli and Marcello Dudovich, Advertising poster for the summer season at the Lido, Treviso, Museo Civico (Collezione Salce, 1931).

di Ca' Pesaro was founded, museums were renovated, professional schools and art academies were founded, and architecture enjoyed a short and very noteworthy period of experimentation just prior to World War I. There were hints of the neo-Byzantine and the Wiener Werkstätten, Josef Hoffmann and Raimondo D'Aronco. These were also the years in which a significant and modern infrastructure began to develop for the accommodation of tourists: beaches and large hotels, travel agencies and banks, shipping companies and yacht clubs. It is precisely in the simultaneous presence of these different and apparently contradictory lines of development that the Venetian experience has been consolidated, showing once again that the city is a complex and modern phenomenon.

But the universal confusion brought about by the war was to interrupt this period of experimentation, shattering illusions and cutting ancient roots. The city still bears significant marks of that season and the years immediately following, including a considerable portion of the "historical" settlement of Lido, which is a handsome little garden city with art-nouveau villas and secession architecture, floral style and art deco, and hotels that seem a hybrid of Côte d'Azur, Brighton, and Cairo. In the city there are period working-class quarters, as well as quite modern ones, residential homes hovering between the ironic neo-Byzantine and decorations by Kolo Moser, quarters on the island of Giudecca in a schematic floral style standing next to Proustian villas with Ravenna-esque encrustations. Since the earliest years of the twentieth century another garden-city has taken root here—the compound of the international pavilions in the Giardini della Biennale, in which nineteenth-century temples of the Muses that seem to have emerged from a painting by Arnold Böcklin coexist with excellent passages of contemporary architecture.

The city and the territory

Following the war, another of the great, controversial projects of Venice was undertaken: the construction of the industrial port on the terra firma in the area around Marghera. This piece of economic history was to have far-reaching effects on the political and economic life of the city, on industrialization and the entrepreneurial class, on social structures, and the city environment: the two-headed beast that comprises insular and historical Venice as well as the Venice of the terra firma, both in its more industrial section and in the rapidly growing residential area of Mestre. Even for historical Venice these developments were key in every area. The fundamental importance of connections with the mainland took center stage; the railroad bridge, and above all the new automotive causeway forced the city to accelerate its efforts to renovate and update its structure. The entire northwestern section of Venice was profoundly affected: the various facilities (garage, parking, bus stops, and so on) of the automotive terminus did not merely stop at the great arrival plaza (Piazzale Roma), but even the network of internal water traffic and that of pedestrian traffic was profoundly influenced and altered. A direct thoroughfare was opened from Piazzale Roma to the center of the city along the Rio Novo, the canal for rapid navigation that leads into the Grand Canal alongside Ca' Foscari. The huge infrastructures of the commercial port of the Marittima join up with the automotive terminus and the railroad station in a vast conglomeration that violently overlies the original grid of the city. At the other end of the city, the facilities of the ancient Arsenale experienced, throughout the nineteenth century and into the twentieth, an ongoing process of updating and expansion that led to its considerable present-day size, leaving a vast area of the city abandoned and useless now that all military and maritime use of the Arsenale has ceased.

53

Aerial view of Venice and the lagoon.

Likewise, at the eastern extremity of Venice there has been a sizable expansion project involving the landfill of the stretch of lagoon beyond the Giardini della Biennale and the construction of the urban quarter of Sant'Elena, the most complete effort to create a totally mimetic and modernized Venetian style. The experiment may not be entirely successful, although there are sections of the quarter that show real architectural quality.

In the period following the Second World War, the dominant theme in Venice seems to involve housing and the inhabitability of the city. Venice had grown during the war due to its more-or-less recognized condition of immunity, and had become unhealthful and lacking in hygienic facilities; a great many dwellings were on the ground floor, and were therefore subject to periodic flooding during high waters. On one hand, the question of housing was important, and on the other hand, increasing attention was paid to such matters as the restoration and conservation of the city's remarkable historical and cultural heritage. Greater and lesser architecture, and the major monuments and works of art—everything appeared to be in progressively greater danger, at risk from transformation and speculation, and inadequate restoration techniques.

Venice in the future

The point of no return appears to have been marked in 1966 by the flood that submerged all of Venice, the islands in the lagoon, and the littoral under an unusual high tide of mud, oil, kerosene, and flotsam. The fragility of Venice is the same as that of much of the Italian territory, which is stressed and threatened by unacceptable phenomena (destruction of the environment and reckless violation of every rule of rational and economic management of resources). In Venice the equilibrium is, if possible, even more precarious, while the quality of the setting and the historical and artistic wealth contained in the city and territory are truly extraordinary. The event of the flooding (and the measures that were thereafter enacted by the national government and local powers, often spurred on by international public opinion) became an occasion to reconsider the role and possible future of the city. It was specifically necessary to rethink method-

ologies for dealing with the complex array of problems weighing upon the city, including the question of a sustainable economic development linked to the industrial town of Marghera, and the issues of mass tourism, both of which increasingly threaten the physical survival of the city. All this is in hope of finding plausible alternatives so that we, and those who come after us, will be able to experience the impossible utopia of Venice.

Walking through this city, seeking its logic, questioning the stone and the marble, the shapes and their gradual deterioration, the

insults that lash this city and the acts of love that heal its sufferings—we see an elusive and ambiguous Venice, an ancient idol, yet contemporary, flexible, and available. Every section and fragment can be linked with another particle or detail. Everything makes sense and all is woven together in the long ribbon of a history that has ended more than once, and begun again just as many times.

Our stroll takes us once again before a wall that bears a marble carving with a Byzantine emperor, amidst four seashells, abandoned like so many leaves of lettuce on a table long since cleared of dishes and silver: the endless mystery of a utopian place reveals and conceals the sense/nonsense of the adventure of free man between the sky and the water of a mud flat that can be transformed into a filthy swamp but which can also glitter with the transparency of a "gem as precious as a stone of crystalline jasper." Everything hangs by a thread: the good will of men.

The center stage of the city: the Platea Sancti Marci

We are all quite familiar with, and perhaps heartily tired of, the interminable series of definitions that have been trotted out in high literature, memoirs and journals, anecdotes, and poetry to describe Piazza San Marco. This immense array of images (some of them effectively original, evocative, romantic, sometimes rhetorical or profoundly critical) constitutes the inevitable point of departure for anyone who ventures across the threshold of the intricate and complex urban structure around the great open space of Piazza San Marco. To begin with, we must take into account the basic elements of the area of Piazza San Marco, or if not basic, then compact or at least unitary. Then we must take them out of context, examine them, and replace them in their proper context. They are a set, a group of architectural structures and spaces, a series of presences and, in some cases, absences, that together drive the huge, intricate machine that is the square. They all work together like a discourse, made up of sentences and words. Linguistically, each of these structures or spaces bears its own highly finished message; but each also expresses a more general overall meaning of the system. There can be no doubt that we are talking about a subject, a remarkable stratification of times and forms coming down to us as the product of a laborious process, unbroken though perhaps discontinuous, here and there contradictory. We cannot forget the other main point of emphasis: this present state of the square is nothing more than a step along the path to new appearances and new dispositions that we cannot even imagine in the present day.

Even the functions and roles of the square and of its individual component parts, and the various substructures of those parts, have undergone radical and continuous shifts both practical and theoretical in nature. The most rapid-fire and fragmentary process of realignment has been that of the functions and messages that cluster around the metaphorical system of "words" and "phrasing" of the square. Equally vigorous has been the transmogrification of roles and the ideological deployment of the structures of the area in relation to the larger universe of signs, meanings, and functions that takes more substantial form in the city of Venice at large. In spite of this, no one can question whether Piazza San Marco constitutes, within this context, a fundamental core of the city (unlike so many other Venetian city-centers, now obsolescent, or long-since replaced by other core structures or areas; among these are Rialto and the Arsenale, the port of San Basilio, or the industrial area of the Giudecca). The edge that gave Piazza San Marco its present-day standing (in prestige, if not in functional terms) is the square's role as the site of the city's main religious shrine and historic political center. Thus, the great political center of Venice survives as a center of myth-making, a continual harvest of historic, artistic, and cultural value.

The term *area marciana* refers to the area around Piazza San Marco. By this term we mean a specific structure, defined in real terms, and we can establish precise boundaries for the area that lies around the ancient Platea Sancti Marci. The structures comprise the basilica and the tripartite system of the *piazze* (Piazza San Marco proper, the Piazzetta di San Marco—set between Palazzo Ducale and the Libreria di San Marco and extending as far as the embankment, or *riva d'acqua*, that is, the Molo—and lastly, the Piazzetta dei Leoncini, on the north side of the basilica). And if one proceeds from the basilica and the buildings that adjoin or overlook it (Longhena's church of San Basso and the nineteenth-century Palazzo Patriarcale) one can soon walk—across a handsome eighteenth-century bridge, the Ponte della Canonica, as if it were a natural extension of the basilica and the piazzetta—over to the old convent of Sant'Apollonia, the original site of the Primicerio di San Marco, the religious authority appointed by the doge who oversaw the basilica. Bounding this structure, overlooking the embankment of the Bacino di San Marco, stands the great mass of the Prigioni Vecchie, which in turn are linked—by the Ponte della Paglia and the famous hanging Bridge of Sighs, or Ponte dei Sospiri—to Palazzo Ducale. The Doge's Palace was the political, juridical, and administrative headquarters of the Venetian Republic; after a certain modern period of use as a city hall and for offices and archives, the Palazzo Ducale has been transformed into a monument proper.

Beyond the piazzetta is the monumental complex that begins with Sansovino's Zecca and then merges into the Libreria di San Marco, and the Procuratie Nuove (completed by Scamozzi and Longhena, and based on the prototype by Sansovino). The western end of Piazza San Marco holds the Ala Napoleonica, then turns at a right angle into the Procuratie Vecchie, and further along concludes with the Torre dell'Orologio. Extending toward the Bacino di San Marco and beyond the Zecca are the exquisite Giardinetti Reali, the product of the demolition of the Gothic granaries at the turn of the nineteenth century. The gardens end at the little marble structure of the Coffee House. Serving as an aquatic terminus immediately behind the Procuratie Vecchie is the Bacino Orseolo, which was created in 1869. The network of structures that extends around the various sectors of the Mercerie is kept at bay by the sharp caesura of the Calle Larga San Marco, another urban backbone and the product of Sansovino's sixteenth-century intervention.

To sum up its perimeters, roughly speaking, the *area marciana* is bounded by the Bacino di San Marco to the south, by the line of Calle Larga San Marco, which continues as far as the Bacino Orseolo to the north, by the thoroughfare that runs from there to the Rio della Luna, swinging past the Coffee House in the Giardinetti to the west, and the area of Prigioni-Sant'Apollonia to the east. This irregular quadrilateral area, about three hundred by two hundred meters (330 by 219 yards), runs north from the great monumental waterfront, and then melts into the dense structural network of the Mercerie and the commercial and residential area of San Giuliano.

Certain free elements claim a status that is anything but secondary in the definition of the whole: the granite columns of Marco and Todaro that serve as an aquatic gateway leading to the Molo, the acritani pillars on the south side of the basilica, the *pietra del bando*, from which decrees were read, also on the basilica's south side; and above all, the campanile (bell tower) with Sansovino's loggetta, which functions as a visual pivot, the ideal center to the entire system, in a sense. Nor should we forget the urban furnishings, the flooring (ranging from that of the basilica to that of the square itself, and even that of the remarkable telescope structure of the Procuratie Nuove), or those more ephemeral elements involved in the buildings' adaptation for active use (ranging from the nineteenth-century cafes to the work done by Carlo Scarpa in the Olivetti store).

The substantial unity of the area that we have just roughly sketched out, although it was always instinctive rather than analytically justifiable, was always accepted—and not only in terms of a functional area. Indeed, the *area marciana* came to exercise an influence on planning, on the popular imagination, and on maintenance and restoration—that is, it came to be a unit of measurement and a filter for the understanding as the single most important piece of

following pages
Basilica di San Marco.

architecture and urban planning in Venetian history. To speak of continuity or discontinuity in relation to such a spatial and temporal setting might seem like so much idle chatter: thus, if the clash between the Libreria and the Zecca is surprising, considering that both were designed under the supervision of Sansovino, it comes as no less of a surprise to note the remarkable degree of harmony in the subsequent planning of the Procuratie Nuove, or the mimetic continuance of the Libreria and Zecca in the Ala Napoleonica. It would appear to be of considerable importance, then, in any description or understanding of the system of St. Mark's, to offer at least a brief reconstruction of the periods and alternating phases that marked—along the course of a considerable stretch of time—the initial formation and ensuing transformation of the architectural organism. This is not only an effort to portray the modifications of the *area marciana* in terms of an orderly succession of architectural vernaculars and styles—it is also an effort to decipher the development of the image and functioning of such an important section of the city. And from this point of view, two emblematic modifications were the major transformations undertaken in this area during the mid-sixteenth century and in the early nineteenth century.

The significance of the basilica and the Palazzo Ducale are unavoidable. Their functions and history, the sedimentation of symbols and rhetoric appear to be capable of overturning roles and hierarchies: consider the Prigioni and the Romantic tradition that enveloped, in a dense mythical aura, the massive stone complex (which is not to mention literary legends of executions, decapitations, escapes—Casanova!—and so forth), or consider the twisted history of the bronze lion that stands proudly atop one of the colossal granite columns near the Molo, and its unfortunate and highly symbolic transfer to Paris during the years of the French occupation of Venice. Consider, lastly, the bell tower, its collapse, and the reasons for that collapse, in 1902, the reconstruction and the strongly ideological debate that distinguished the process of rebuilding, and its inauguration in 1912. It is well known that until the thirteenth century Piazza San Marco was much smaller than it is now: a canal (traces of which can still be seen in the sewerworks beneath the pavement) split the area in two. The oldest building in the complex is the basilica, even though the present-day Basilica di San Marco is the third one documented, and has been transformed in its exterior appearance by the addition of Gothic ornaments and modern mosaics.

Palazzo Ducale is similarly the result of the reconstruction of a far earlier fortified building. It united in a single structure both the headquarters of the government and the hall of justice, as well as the residence of the doge and the city prison. Damaged by a number of fires, particularly the fire of 1576, the building was reconstructed to harmonize with the existing *area marciana* after the rejection of a plan by Palladio to rebuild it in the "modern" style.

The profound modification of Piazza San Marco by Jacopo Sansovino, or at least at his specific indication, dates back to just before 1450. At that time the campanile (bell tower) was left isolated (earlier it had been incorporated in the curtain wall of the southern front of the square), and the Molo, the piazzetta, and the piazza proper took on their present-day form. A number of formal and stylistic considerations determined new axes and new semantics: the classical, antiquarian language of the Libreria (with its problems, exquisitely typical of the Renaissance, concerning the proper use of orders), the strategic location of the loggetta at the base of the campanile, the intentionally dissonant connection between the Libreria and the Zecca or between the Libreria and the Procuratie Nuove. These and other subjects fascinated scholars, and added learned treatises and essays to violent ideological disagreements and political factionalism: pro-papal, pro-imperial, Francophiles; in favor of a rigid or a flexible oligarchy, in favor of an institutionalized immobility, or in favor of reforms. Around the turn of the sixteenth century, the decision to build the Torre dell'Orologio and the Procuratie Vecchie clearly indicated a tendency toward a continuous architectural vocabulary, favoring an autonomy that was also in tune with the cultural self-sufficiency of which the city was so proud—a self-sufficiency that was destined to succumb to the rediscovered architectural language of Rome, both ancient and modern.

Another, deep-rooted renovation occurred at the fall of the Venetian Republic. The erection in 1797 of the revolutionary and republican Tree of Liberty, in imitation of the French example marked the end of a paralysis in Venice caused by the heavy hand of a long-decrepit ancien régime, but it opened the way to institutional adventures, as well as architectural and urbanistic experiments that were

not always of the highest quality. The Piazza San Marco was transformed, with the demolition of the shorter wall, to make way for a monumental staircase leading up to the official reception area of the new (from 1807 on) Napoleonic palace which later became the Hapsburg palace. On the Molo the old Gothic Granai (grain siloes) were demolished in 1807 to make way for a garden (the Giardinetti

Reali) and for the construction of a number of small pavilions for the use of the court. And in the 1840s, in the place of a number of venerable old residences alongside the Basilica di San Marco, the residence of the Patriarch was built.

From that time on, other transformations have altered the old heart of the city. Consider the introduction of gas lighting in 1843,

the conversion of the old taverns into handsome cafes in the nine-teenth and twentieth centuries, the expulsion of the various goods shops, from butchers to cobblers to wig-vendors, to make way for shops selling knick-knacks and souvenirs to tourists. Above all, there has been a radical change in the people using what the architects of the sixteenth century meant as something like an ancient Forum, the space that in the eighteenth century was decorated as a giant carpet, that Napoleon wished to use as the setting for his imperial epiphany, that the bourgeoisie loved as a great drawing room for displaying its own little vanities, that witnessed oceanic crowds during the Fascist era, and which finally celebrated, with civic and moral dignity, its joy at the return to liberty in 1945.

Basilica di San Marco (St. Mark's Cathedral)

Erected by the Partecipazio family to function as a city church, the original structure was rebuilt under Doge Pietro Orseolo the Holy after the fire of 976. The present-day building was begun in 1063 under the Contarini doge-ship on the model of the Imperial Basilica of the Holy Apostles in Constantinople. It was built to house the remains of Saint Mark, which were stolen from Alexandria, Egypt by Venetian merchants in A.D. 828, and in time it came to serve as a Palatine chapel, adjacent to the headquarters of the doge. The sumptuous facade is completed by a Hellenistic group of horses—loot from the siege of Constantinople in 1204—and is distinguished by three portals. The central portal consists of three large concentric arches, decorated on the exterior and interior by marble reliefs, once richly colored with gold and light blue. Benedetto Antelami's series of Romanesque sculptures in the cathedrals of the Po Valley are quoted here in simplified forms by Venetian craftsmen from the same period.

Begun to a typically Byzantine conception in 1063 under the Doge Domenico Contarini, the basilica has remained essentially unchanged in its internal architectural lines. The wall facings in rare marble originally from the East were begun by the Doge Vitale Michiel II in the twelfth century, as were the famous mosaics that have won this church the name of Basilica d'Oro, or Cathedral of Gold. This building has a central plan based on a Greek cross, with a main nave, and two smaller aisles surmounted by galleries. The Cupola dell'Ascensione, set between the nave and the transept, dates from the thirteenth century and depicts Christ in a golden robe giving a benediction (opposite). The mosaics, the earliest of which show the influence of Ravenna, developed a more proper Venetian style between the twelfth and thirteenth centuries. In a mixture of flamboyant Gothic, Renaissance, and mannerism, this building features the work of Giambono and Paolo Uccello as well as Andrea del Castagno, Tintoretto, and Jacopo Palma the Younger. The mosaics of polychrome marble that wind along the structure of the church feature two quite distinct techniques: the opus tessellatum, composed of tiles of different sizes but all cut in the same regular fashion; and the opus sectile which makes use of small, irregular fragments of different stones, used especially for zoomorphic and geometric motifs. The Gothic iconostasis of red broccatello Veronese marble, dating from 1394, divides the hall from the presbytery. Set on an architrave surmounted by a silver cross are arranged the Virgin Mary, Saint John the Evangelist, and the twelve apostles, in bronze sculptures by Jacobello and Pierpaolo Delle Masegne (below). The Cappella Zen, lavishly decorated between 1504 and 1521 by Antonio Lombardo, Paolo Savin, and by the caster Paolo Campanato, was built in honor of the Cardinal Giambattista Zen, nephew of Pope Paul II. In virtue of a considerable bequest to the Venetian Republic, Zen succeeded in obtaining burial in the chapel.

65

Palazzo Ducale

The celebratory and propagandistic intentions of the Venetian Republic are clearly exemplified in this building by centuries of art that exalt the most glorious moments of the Venetian epic. Legions of artists, including Titian, Veronese, Tintoretto, Pisanello, and Vittoria, contributed to the spectacular decoration of this sanctuary of Republican virtues, which was also the gallows of traitors, or supposed traitors, such as the Doge Marin Faliero.

The existing building was begun at the end of the thirteenth century, and was completed during the reign of the Doge Francesco Foscari in 1438. The lightness of the palazzo's elevations, rich in ogival fretwork, makes this a masterpiece of Gothic art. Headquarters of the doge and of the various magistracies of the state, it served as a judicial tribunal and as a prison, and was the symbol of the Serenissima itself. Nothing survives of the original Byzantine building—a stronghold with a square plan,

defended at the corners by towers, and entered through fortified portals— which was built in the eleventh century by the Partecipazio family. The present-day structure is the product of a late-thirteenth-century reconstruction, which rose around the Sala del Maggior Consiglio. Between 1340 and 1365 the wing of the palazzo toward the Molo was rebuilt, and the elevation, completed in 1419, took on its present-day appearance with three horizontal bands. The reversal of volumes was revolutionary:

up high was the "solid" with its polychrome facing; in the center was the harmonious succession of the continual loggia and the inflected arches with four-lobed fretwork; at the bottom was a pointed-arch portico, supported by sunken columns. It is said that the stonecutter Filippo Calendario designed the portico, creating a prototype that in time spread through Gothic Venice. The series of windows in the middle, which mix local styles with an Arabian, geometric motif, was to become a

typological constant in Venetian architecture. At the beginning of the fifteenth century, the façade overlooking the embankment had its large central window embellished with spires and sculptures, creations of the Dalle Masegne family. In 1424 the side overlooking the Piazzetta di San Marco was completed, sealed in 1442 by the late-Gothic touch of the Porta della Carta by Bartolomeo Bon, a member of a renowned dynasty of stonecutters; the Bons and the Ravertis worked together on this last

68

major modification to the exterior of this building. The courtyard originally contained, in what were to become the porticoes that punctuate its perimeter, stables, guard houses, servants' quarters, and prisons. The superb late-Gothic and Renaissance transformation between 1483 and 1489 made this a reception area for the powers that ruled Venice, culminating in the two exceedingly ornate bronze well heads made by Alfonso Alberghetti and Niccolò De Conti between 1554 and 1559.

The Scala dei Giganti (stairway of giants), the ceremonial entryway to the Sale Palatine (palace halls, far left), is splendidly adorned with rare marble-work, reliefs, niello-work, and allegorical scenes. Looming powerfully over it are the two giant sculptures of Mars and Neptune by Jacopo Sansovino, symbols of Venice's commercial dominance and rule over the seas. Upon the stairway, built by Antonio Rizzo, head builder of the palazzo between 1483 and 1489, the coronation of the doge regularly took place.

The Scala d'Oro, or stairway of gold (middle), which rises to the interior from the courtyard, also reiterates the powerful symbolic message of the Venetian Signoria, with Alessandro Vittoria's late-sixteenth-century, mannerist, white-and-gilt stuccoes, and allegorical frescoes by Battista Franco.

The succession of halls on the interior contains a treasure of paintings and decoration. The Sala del Collegio, designed by Palladio in 1574 and built by Antonio da Ponte, features sumptuous furnishings and wooden finishings, and a ceiling dominated by the Apotheosis of Venice (opposite), a painting by Paolo Veronese. On the side walls the history of Venice continues to provide the subject of the pictorial narrative. The participation of the Serenissima through the person of the Doge Ziani in the rivalry between Pope Alexander III and the Emperor Frederick Barbarossa was one of the first Venetian actions in the field of politics (bottom). And the splendid history of the Republic of Venice is once again the subject of the sixteenth-century late-mannerist canvas (below) by Andrea Vicentino, which depicts Henri III, king of France and Poland, being greeted by the Doge Alvise Mocenigo and by the Patriarch Giovanni Trevisan at San Niccolò al Lido in 1574. The canvas—the work of an artist who belonged to the so-called Scuola delle Sette Maniere (school of the seven manners) particularly active in the Palazzo Ducale following the great fires of 1574 and 1577—depicts the great festivities held by the Republic in honor of the young king of Valois, culminating in a banquet that had as its remarkable setting the Sala del Maggior Consiglio. One can glimpse the triumphal arch that Palladio erected at the Lido for the arrival of the monarch who, won over by the splendor and generosity of the Serenissima, prolonged his stay long past his planned departure.

Procuratie Vecchie

On the northern side of Piazza San Marco there extends—broken only on a line with the Torre dell'Orologio—the compact structure of the Procuratie Vecchie. The building, which extends 152 meters (166 yards) in length, clearly took inspiration from the Veneto-Byzantine tradition of building. Rising above a ground-floor portico, comprising an arcade of fifty arches that now house shops, there rises a double order of elegant round-arch windows. Traditionally attributed to Mauro Codussi, the construction of the Procuratie, which extended from 1500 to 1532, is now thought to have been the work of Antonio Abbondi, known as the Scarpagnino. This latter architect was quite active in sixteenth-century Venice. He worked on the churches of San Sebastiano, Santo Spirito, and San Fantin, he took part in the reconstruction of the Rialto area following the terrible fire, and he worked on the construction of the Palazzo Ducale and the Scuola Grande di San Rocco.

72

Palazzo Patriarcale

When the patriarchal see was transferred in 1807 to San Marco from its original location in San Pietro di Castello, it became necessary to provide a new headquarters for the religious authority of Venice near the Basilica di San Marco, which was now no longer a ducal chapel, but the city cathedral. At the same time, a final version was being completed of the Piazzetta dei Leoncini, a site that linked the northern side of the basilica with the Palazzo Ducale. Lorenzo Santi, after having come up with some twenty design ideas, opted in 1836 for a decidedly neoclassical style, an absolutely new and unprecedented presence in the continuum of the Platea Marciana, and an ideal conclusion of the Napoleonic project, which had already been under construction for some three decades. Completed in 1850, this palazzo contains what was once the Sala dei Banchetti, or banquet hall of the Signoria; one once entered this hall from the Palazzo Ducale via a hanging passageway. Built by Bartolomeo Manopola between 1618 and 1623, the building was transformed into its present-day version by Bernardo Maccaruzzi around 1750, when it was adorned with frescoes and paintings by Jacopo Guarana, Francesco Zanchi, and Nicolò Bambini.

Set between the Platea Marciana and the Mercerie, a major commercial thoroughfare, this clock tower with its vertical progression through three orders, rich in polychrome and gilt decorations, serves as a hinge for the larger area. Designed and built by Mauro Codussi between 1496 and 1499, it features two wings on either side, the work of Pietro Lombardo in 1506; these are crowned by a terrace that was added by Giorgio Massari in 1755. The large clock, enameled in dark blue and gold, dates to 1499, and marks the time, the phases of the moon, and the phases of the stars. Above the niche that contains a statue of the Virgin Mary stands the proud lion of St. Mark, while the two bronze statues of the Mori—or Moors, so called for their dark hue—cast by Ambrogio Da Le Anchore in 1497 to a design by Paolo Savin, have for centuries marked the hours by hammering the large central bell mounted on the rooftoop terrace.

The construction of this loggetta formed part of the program for the renovation of the Saint Mark's area, which involved the Libreria and the Zecca, also by Jacopo Sansovino. The loggetta, set at the base of the campanile, shades the contrast between the vertical lines of the bell tower and the predominantly horizontal cast of the buildings surrounding the square. A triumphal arch that proclaimed the Venetian acquisition of the heritage of ancient Rome, this structure represented the triumph of the aristocratic class, whose destinies were identified with that of the Republic itself. Built between 1537 and 1542 to plans by Sansovino, it immediately won favorable mention from Pietro Aretino and sanctioned the full-fledged entry of the ars antiqua into the most prestigious site in Venice. Eight polychrome marble columns set on high bases support a trabeation and frame the three entrance arches. The trifore, or three-section windows, on the side elevations, an homage to the Lombard tradition, impart lightness to the architecture. Statues of pagan gods along with the allegorical bas-reliefs in the upper section constitute a rhetorical artifice in a montage of citations. In this Olympus, evoked in praise of Republican virtues, the sole trace of Christianity is the statue of the Virgin Mary, likewise by Sansovino. In 1663 the terrace was added, and in 1749, after having been used as the headquarters of the Banco del Lotto, or bank of the lottery, it was restored by Giorgio Massari and badly altered with other arbitrary restorations by the Gai family. Destroyed in 1902 by the collapse of the campanile, it was rebuilt with the original materials and elements.

The renovation of the city ordered by Doge Andrea Gritti began in 1536 with the construction of the Zecca, or mint. Jacopo Sansovino, master builder in charge of construction around San Marco, demolished the old building, in which money had been coined since 1227, and built a new, more massive and powerful building. Rusticated semi-columns, Doric on the second floor and Ionic on the third, and broad windows with triangular pediments, punctuate the facade overlooking the Bacino di San Marco, atop the rusticated ground floor.

The Libreria, too, was built by Sansovino between 1537 and 1554 at the orders of the Procuratori di San Marco, as a site for the storage of the books of the Venetian Republic, including the exquisite Byzantine codices brought to Venice by Cardinal Bessarione in 1468. It still houses the Biblioteca Marciana and features such treasures as the fifteenth-century Grimani Breviary and various editions by Aldus Manutius. The building is an elongated loggia punctuated by two stacked orders of Doric and Ionic semi-columns. On the second

floor is the Vestibule designed by Vincenzo Scamozzi in 1597, with a trompe-l'oeil ceiling featuring Titian's Wisdom. The Sala Dorata (Gilded Room), whose walls are decorated with a series of philosophers, may be considered the first expression of the "new" mannerist style of painting in Venice. Its spectacular wooden ceiling features twenty-one tondoes, the result of a remarkable competition among seven artists, conceived by Titian and Sansovino and won by Paolo Veronese.

Ala Napoleonica and Museo Correr

Set in the Procuratie Nuove, the Palazzo Reale (royal palace)—the greatest architectural creation of the neoclassical period in Venice—was meant to serve as an emblem of Napoleon's power in the ultimate symbolic site of the ancient Venetian Republic: the Platea Marciana. Giovanni Antolini (soon replaced by Giuseppe Soli and Lorenzo Santi, who were summoned in 1807 to work at the court of the viceroy Eugene Beauharnais) hoped that the demolition of Sansovino's church of San

Geminiano would give a unified appearance to the square, as well as offer space to the reception areas of the new regime, such as the immense staircase and the halls on the piano nobile, including the ambitious ballroom. Built by Lorenzo Santi between 1810 and 1813, this ballroom extends between two hemicyles with half-cupolas and Corinthian columns in white and gold. The hall and its original furnishings were designed by Giuseppe Borsato, the central figure of the neoclassical style

in Venice. Since 1922, this palazzo has housed the Museo Correr, comprising the notable collections that the patrician Teodoro Correr bequeathed to the city upon his death in 1830. Along with souvenirs and memorabilia of the Republic and a notable numismatic collection, there are fine art masterpieces, including sculptures by Antonio Canova, paintings by Lorenzo Veneziano, the Bellini family, Carpaccio, Antonello da Messina, the Flemish masters, and the school of Ferrara.

Before the international Gothic

Church of Santi Maria e Donato
(Virgin Mary and San Donato),
Murano. Detail of the mosaic floor.

Ca' da Mosto

This is one of the most venerable patrician residences along the Grand Canal, dating back to the twelfth or thirteenth century. While two stories were added to the building in the seventeenth and eighteenth centuries, it is still possible to perceive the forms of the Veneto-Byzantine palazzo-fondaco in the two lower stories. In the elegant sequence on the second floor, the agile cusped extrados already seem to allude to the Venetian Gothic style. The marble sheathing on this level is encrusted by paterae in relief, and bounded by a horizontal marcapiano (the stringcourse marking the height of the story). The off-center portico on the ground floor probably dates from the eleventh century, and may well have been used at first as a storehouse. The da Mosto family, originally from Padua, earned distinction as skilled sailors, and were admitted to the Venetian aristocracy in 1292. The family sold the palazzo at the end of the sixteenth century, and in 1661 it became the site of the most luxurious Venetian hotel of the time of the Republic, called the Leon Bianco (White Lion). Among its guests was the Austro-Hungarian emperor Josef II, who declined the official hospitality of the Serenissima in 1769 and 1775, preferring to stay in the hotel. There were also the "Counts of the North," the registered names of the Czarevitch Paul and the Czarevna Feodorovna, future czar and czarina of the Russias. The couple was at the heart of an unrivaled season of balls and spectacles, offered in fierce competition by Venice's aristocracy.

Palazzo Barziza

By the twelfth century, the typology of the aristocratic home in Venice had already assumed the physiognomy that it was largely to retain over the centuries that followed. This home was not merely a dwelling; it also tended to be the site of commerce and trade, and the ground floor of the great palazzi had a huge entryway with a portico leading directly onto the canal. Here goods were loaded and unloaded to and from gondolas and lighters. Although alterations have been made over the centuries that will forever change its appearance, Palazzo Barziza still presents numerous features redolent of the Veneto-Byzantine school of architecture of the twelfth and thirteenth centuries. Along with the paterae that dot the masonry, note the nicely decorated portal and the course of mullioned windows on the third floor between arches with exquisite cusped extrados.

Palazzo Loredan and Palazzo Farsetti

Despite the fact that both these buildings, begun in the twelfth century, have been raised by two stories, they still display a distinct characteristic of the Veneto-Byzantine style: a continual loggia extending the length of the facade of the piano nobile, or main floor, and a portico on the ground floor, with fortified pillars on either side. It is traditionally said that Ca' Loredan—which has been the site of the city-government offices of Venice since 1868—was built by the Boccasi family, originally from Parma; it later belonged to the Ziani family and later still to the Corner family. In 1362 the Corner family fêted the King of Cyprus in great luxury, as an honored guest (his royal coat of arms can still be seen on the upper loggia). As a token of his appreciation, the king invested Federico Corner with the prized fiefdom of Piscopia. Born in this palazzo in 1646 was Elena Lucrezia Cornaro Piscopia, the first woman in the world to take a college degree, from the university of Padua in 1678. In 1703, due to inheritance by marriage, the building became the property of the Loredan family, whose name it still bears. The facade, altered in the sixteenth century, is punctuated at the ground floor by a portico with five arches, flanked by two twinned windows, separated by sections of solid wall. The loggia on the second story is comprised of arches with imposts on the capitals of the slender columns, two of them twinned as a notation of the solid-wall division on the interior. Coats of arms and Gothic reliefs in marble adorn the spandrel of each arch.

Palazzo Loredan's twin is Ca' Farsetti, which now houses offices of the city government. It presents the same magnificent Byzantine progression of features, varying only in the twin columns that support the arches of the loggia. Once the residence of the aristocratic Dandolo family, which produced the celebrated Doge Enrico Dandolo who conquered Constantinople in the first years of the thirteenth century during the Fourth Crusade, this building came into the hands of the Farsetti family as late as 1669, five years after their admission into the nobility of Venice. In the eighteenth century, Filippo Farsetti took advantage of his immense wealth and his position of prestige following the election as pope of his cousin Carlo Rezzonico, and bedecked the palazzo with an immense collection of copies of classical statues. In the early eighteenth century, the building became the Accademia Farsetti, an arts academy that served as the chief point of diffusion for the neoclassical school of art in Venice. Among the many artists that studied here was the young Antonio Canova, who enrolled in 1768; his first sculptural effort—two baskets of flowers and fruit, now in the Museo Correr—were once displayed on the great staircase of Ca' Farsetti.

Palazzo Lion Morosini

Dating back to the thirteenth century, Ca' Lion overlooks a small yard, or campiello—known as the Campiello del Remer—overlooking the Grand Canal. The old building, though heavily renovated, still preserves its original structure as a residence with warehouse and storefront wrapped around a courtyard. On the outer facade of the piano nobile, where the windows and the portal with its exquisite cornice are redolent of a Veneto-Byzantine style marked by Eastern accents, note the exterior staircase, which leads to the residential floor above the area where merchandise was stored. The solid form of the staircase wall incised with pointed arches on the ground floor contrasts with the light Gothic of the flight on the left. Built for the Lioni family, the palazzo was later the property of the Morosini family, and still bears the names of both families.

Palazzo Falier Canossa

A Gothic construction of the mid-fourteenth century, this palazzo was later rebuilt with the addition of two loggiaed forewings—themselves renovated in the nineteenth century—which extend from the main elevation. An elegant ogival pentafore, or five-section window, adorns the facade, which features a Gothic portal. The most infamous member of the Falier family was the Doge Marino Falier, who was beheaded in 1354 for plotting to take absolute power. He lived in Palazzo ai Santi Apostoli.

Corte Bottera

Not far from the Campo San Zanipolo, if one climbs the first few steps of the Ponte Storto, it is possible to enter a narrow, private fondamenta *that leads into the Corte Bottera. This is a secluded corner in the labyrinthine grid of the Sestiere di Castello, almost inevitably ignored by the crowds of tourists visiting the enormous, neighboring Dominican church of Santi Giovanni e Paolo. Archaic structural elements, such as the immense thirteenth- to fourteenth-century Veneto-Byzantine*

portal adorned with plant and animal motifs, and the fourteenth-century porticoed exterior stairway, compete with the fifteenth-century late-Gothic stylized well head to create a spot of picturesque charm.

Basilica di Santa Maria Assunta, on Torcello

Gone forever are the palazzi, churches, homes, and convents that populated the island of Torcello in the years of its splendor, when more than ten thousand people lived here. The island is now almost completely deserted. Among the few relics of its past stands the Basilica of Santa Maria Assunta (Our Lady of the Assumption), founded in the eighth century, but rebuilt in its present-day form in 1008, when Orso Orseolo, son of the Doge Pietro Orseolo, was made bishop of Torcello. The Veneto-Byzantine building has a basilican plan; in front is a colonnaded portico that was enlarged in the fifteenth century. The alluring interior hall, split in three parts by a double line of columns and culminating in the apse with the high podium of the choir loft, is closed off by an iconostasis with six little columns and Byzantine plutei topped by fifteenth-century panels depicting the Virgin Mary and the Apostles. The real wonder of this basilica, however, lies in the rich marble-inlay floors and the rare array of mosaics on the walls and vaults.

The mosaics are a meeting ground for two different schools: the Veneto-Byzantine school, and the school of Ravenna; the latter was more closely tied to tradition. While the regal Mother and Child standing against the gold background of the apse is in the rigid Byzantine vernacular of Ravenna, the mosaic above the main door, the Apotheosis of Christ and the Last Judgment, clearly seeks another narrative tradition, especially in its depiction of the damned, with a timid realism that is more deeply

Venetian. This mosaic was probably begun in the eleventh century, and was completed shortly after the middle of the twelfth century. According to documents dating back to 1153 there were Greek master mosaicists at work in the Basilica, including a certain Marcus Indriomenis.

There is still a small window in the basilica (page 93, top) that is shuttered, as it has been since construction of the church, by a diaphanous slab of alabaster hung on hinges. The diffuse lighting that filters through it is that

tenuous and suspended illumination that is distinctly typical of the older Venetian churches from the earliest period of the republic.

Church of San Zan Degolà (San Giovanni Decollato, or Saint John Beheaded)

The interior of this exceedingly old church—founded between the seventh and eighth centuries—still shows its origins as a Veneto-Byzantine basilica, despite the modifications that have occurred over time. The church is divided up into a nave and two aisles, with a ship's-keel ceiling that dates back to the eleventh century. Other elements from the same stylistic vein are the cushion capitals of the Greek-marble columns, supporting pointed arches. The exterior dates to the turn of the eighteenth century, and has a tripartite elevation corresponding to the layout of the interior. The paintings here consist largely of fifteenth-century frescoes. Especially noteworthy are the very rare frescoes depicting saints, the work of the Byzantine school of the thirteenth or fourteenth century located in the chapel to the left of the apse. Over the access arch leading into this apse is a thirteenth-century mosaic of the Annunciation (opposite, bottom).

96

Church of San Giacometto (San Giacomo a Rialto)

This church was one of very few buildings in the Rialto area to survive the terrible fire of 1514. Named after St. James, San Giacomo—or San Giacometto, as it has been fondly nicknamed by the Venetians because of its diminutive size—was first constructed in the twelfth century, and it retains its original appearance. The unassuming facade is embellished with a portico dating back to the fourteenth century; atop it stands a campanile. The interior is laid out on a Greek-cross plan comprising three aisles flanked by columns of Greek marble, with eleventh-century Veneto-Byzantine capitals. The church was renovated in the seventeenth century, and contains paintings by Leandro Bassano and Marco Vecellio, and a Pietà that has been attributed to Carlo Dolci. The Altare degli Orefici was designed by Vincenzo Scamozzi and is adorned by bronze figures by Gerolamo Campagna. The marble statue of the patron saint on the main altar is the work of Alessandro Vittoria.

Church of San Giacomo dell'Orio

This church dates back to 1225 but may first have been founded in the ninth century. It was originally built to a basilican plan of clear Byzantine influence, and a three-aisle transept was added between the fourteenth and fifteenth centuries. The interior combines the Romanesque style with pointed arches, and is dominated by a three-lobed wooden ship's-keel ceiling, set on corbels and marked at the center by a cable weave, a fourteenth-century creation by Venetian master craftsmen. Veneto-Byzantine reliefs and paterae, Gothic sculptures and paintings by Francesco Bassano, Andrea Meldolla Schiavone, Lorenzo Lotto, Jacopo Palma the Younger, Giovanni Buonconsiglio, and Paolo Veronese—who also painted five panels in the ceiling of the sacristy—enrich this house of worship. An Ionic column, of a single piece of verde antico brought from Byzantium serves as a counterpoint to the Anatolian marble of the holy water stoup and the entry portal.

Church of Santi Maria e Donato (Virgin Mary and San Donato) on Murano

This church, founded by the earliest inhabitants of the lagoon in the seventh century, was transformed and enlarged on a basilican plan after the year 1000. The stern facade is derived from examples in Ravenna; at the base of the side piers, note the Roman plaques from the second century A.D. featuring strong portraits. Along the sides and on the outside of the apse of this church, the radical restoration carried out by Camillo Boito between 1858 and 1873 took the original facies down to brick; it is enlivened by large splayed niches, and is crowned by a double series of small arches. The interior, split into three sections by a double line of columns, has a high transept and a wooden ship's-keel roof dating from the early fifteenth century. Artworks by Lazzaro Bastiani and Marco Vecellio and a painting attributed to Paolo Veneziano surround the frescoes in the style of Giotto in the apse; above them, set on a gold background, is the Madonna Orante, or Virgin Mary Praying, a Byzantine mosaic dating from the twelfth century. The marvelous mosaic floor in the Veneto-Byzantine style was executed in two different techniques: the opus vermiculatum, composed of marble and glass paste in brilliant colors, and the opus sectile, made up exclusively of stone. It dates back to 1140, making it contemporary with the flooring of the Basilica di San Marco.

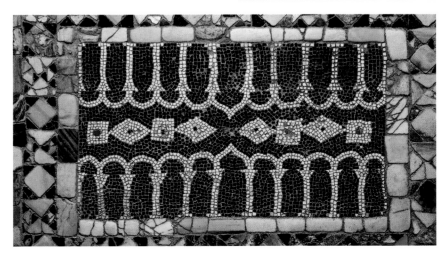

This church, founded in the earliest times—tradition dates it to the eighth century—was rebuilt in the twelfth century. It stands out of the way, far from the economic and political centers of Venice, in a quarter traditionally of the less well-to-do. For this reason, it managed to pass through the centuries with relatively few and minor modifications, especially on the exterior, which still features a brick, shed-roof façade, covered in part by a fifteenth-century portico intended for the devotional use of the pinzochere, poor Venetian Beguines who were wholly devoted to prayer. The interior, with a nave and two aisles, features a central apse with a Veneto-Byzantine cornice dating back to the reconstruction in the twelfth century. Around 1580 the interior walls of the nave were faced with a late-mannerist ornamental covering made up of canvases, carved gilt wooden elements, and holy sculptures. At the same time a new iconostasis was built, and a flat ceiling with panels painted by artists from the milieu of Paolo Veronese, namely Francesco Montemezzano and Leonardo Corona, depicting episodes of the life of Christ.

Cloister of Sant'Apollonia

The thirteenth-century cloister of Santa Scolastica, better known under the name of Sant'Apollonia, is the oldest cloister in the city. It is concealed just a short distance from the bustling Piazza San Marco. This structure, which clearly shows the influence of the Romanesque styles from the terra firma, is a unique occurrence in the art history of the Serenissima. The cloister is ringed with short columns—single columns on two sides, and twinned on the other two sides—set on a continuous base, supporting rounded terracotta, ashlared arches of varying heights and widths. Veneto-Byzantine influence can be seen in the capitals and the central well head, introducing a more profound local note into an avowedly Romanesque environment. The cloister, which has survived intact to the present day despite a major modification to make it taller in the eighteenth century, led into the old Benedictine nunnery, which is believed to date back to the twelfth or thirteenth century. In 1473 the monastery passed under the jurisdiction of the Primicerio di San Marco, the highest religious authority of the Cappella Ducale, and became the headquarters of the Primicerio. From 1579 to 1591 the Seminario Ducale, a seminary school, was housed here, and under Hapsburg rule in 1828 it was adapted as the Imperial Regio Tribunale Criminale, a criminal court, with a revision of the facade by the architect Lorenzo Santi. On the outside walls of the cloister—restored beginning in 1964 by the Procuratoria di San Marco—is a collection of Roman, Byzantine, and proto-Venetian finds from the Lapidario Marciano. The second floor houses the Museo della Basilica Marciana.

The Gothic style: civil and religious

Palazzo Ducale.
Detail of the loggia overlooking the piazzetta.

Ca' d'Oro

This elegant Gothic palazzo takes its name from the gilding that once adorned its marble, which is now restored to its original polychrome splendor through a careful restoration. Built between 1421 and 1423 on behalf of Marino Contarini by master builders and craftsmen who had previously worked in the Palazzo Ducale, this building was in part the creation of the Raverti and the Bon families, two of the dynasties of stonecutters who were originally responsible for the creation of Gothic Venice. The virtuosity of the architecture, the prevalence of empty space over solid stone, the lacy embroidery of the intricate stone fretwork, the spectacular marble inlay and carvings: all these features make the Ca' d'Oro the unrivaled masterpiece of Venetian Gothic architecture. The breadth of the Gothic courtyard is punctuated by the customary hanging staircase, set on arches typical of the native Venetian pointed-arch style, and is anchored by the wellhead by Bartolomeo Bon (page 110). Since 1927, the palazzo has housed a notable art collection assembled by and named for Giorgio Franchetti, who donated it to the city of Venice. The first thing Franchetti did upon ownership of the building was eliminate the fanciful restorations and neo-Gothic pastiches added by Giambattista Meduna after 1840 when the palazzo was the property of Maria Taglioni, the most celebrated dancer of the time. Franchetti's collection included an eclectic group of paintings, bronzes, marble sculptures, and wooden polyptychs, Gothic and Renaissance furniture, Flemish tapestries, and numerous fifteenth-century medals, including several by Pisanello (Antonio Pisano) and Gentile Bellini.

Enlarged by more recent acquisitions and reordered and renovated in accordance with modern museum criteria, the collection today includes works from Venice, surrounding areas, and elsewhere: sculptures by Jacopo Sansovino, the Lombardi (Pietro and sons Tullio and Antonio), and Alessandro Vittoria; bronze figurines by Andrea Briosco, sketches by Gianlorenzo Bernini and Antonio Canova, and paintings by Titian, Anthony Van Dyck, and Mantegna. Titian and Giorgione's renowned frescoes completed in 1508 for the facade of the Fondaco dei Tedeschi were also brought here after being detached from the Fondaco in 1967.

Andrea Mantegna painted the jewel of the collection. Set in a marble aedicule, Mantegna's Saint Sebastian (opposite) was commissioned by Luigi Gonzaga around 1500. Far from the idealization that is so much a part of the Central Italian Renaissance, and the exquisite balance of Giovanni Bellini and Leonardo da Vinci, Mantegna was in search of his own highly dramatic form of expression profoundly linked to the Po valley. His compact and deeply modeled shapes stand out, not against neo-Platonic landscapes, but against an impenetrable dark background.

110

Calle del Paradiso

The name of this street—Heavenly Way—is a reference to the public illuminations that were held here every Good Friday during the Venetian Republic; the calle itself is a fine example of medieval construction. Flanked on either side by working-class row housing, along the ground floors of which one can still see the pillars and wooden architraves of the doors to the old workshops, the street is narrowed even more by the sharply projecting walls of the second stories, set upon solid corbel brackets. At the corner on the water stand two thirteenth-century buildings whose facades feature elements of Veneto-Byzantine architecture, mixed with other, Gothic features, dating back to the reconstruction done by the abbot of Pomposa, who owned them in the early fifteenth century. The two palazzetti then became property of the Foscari and the Mocenigo families; in time they were joined by a flamboyant Gothic arch. In this arch, beneath a lovely cusp adorned with a four-lobe oculus, is the Virgin Mary, originally sheltering under her mantle one youth from each family, with their heraldic crests. This commemorated an alliance by marriage. A simpler arch anchors the calle at the other end.

Palazzo Ariani

This palazzo dates back to the second half of the fourteenth century; the facade on the top floor contains the original windows. This lovely loggia constitutes the first appearance of the fretwork window in Venetian Gothic architecture; the highest manifestation of this typology was to come in the Palazzo Ducale. This structural feature—an airy intertwining of geometric lines, arches, and scrollwork was to become a constant presence, embellishing the facades of Venice's patrician dwellings. The great families of stonecutters, the De Santis, Bon, Raverti, and Dalle Masegne worked tirelessly at the stone of Venice, making it airy and light as filigree. Above the pointed arches extends an exquisite ornamental motif, clearly of Eastern origin. Typical elements of Venetian Gothic architecture remain the asymmetric facade linked to the interior layout of the rooms, and the corner portico with the roofed staircase, which can be reached from the walled courtyard.

Palazzo Fortuny
(Palazzo Pesaro degli Orfei)

Proudly separate from the other buildings overlooking the Campo San Beneto, the grim and almost medieval Gothic elevation of Palazzo Pesaro degli Orfei—named after an eighteenth-century philharmonic academy that met here—did not undergo the fanciful "picturesque" renovations during the nineteenth century that so altered other buildings from the period. Even the Gothic layout of the interior is still intact, thanks to the intelligent approach to restoration taken by the last private owner of the palazzo, Mariano Fortuny y Madrazo, painter and stage designer for Richard Wagner. The only things altering the original spaces are theatrical fabrics and drapery produced in the artist's workshops; those workshops once occupied the third story of this building, but now they are located at the Giudecca. The decadent interior is replete with classical casts, copies, and paintings by Fortuny himself, bronze figurines, musical instruments, sofas covered with velvets and brocades, all lit by theatrical lamps designed by the endlessly creative Fortuny.

Palazzo Pisani Moretta

This late-Gothic building enlivened by spacious loggiaed windows was built in the fifteenth century. It bears the name Moretta because it belonged to a branch of the Pisani family that descended in the fourteenth century from a certain Almorò, whose name evolved over the centuries into Moretta. Inside the palazzo—perfectly preserved by the aristocratic family that now owns it—a majestic staircase built by Andrea Tirali leads to the piano nobile, where, between 1739 and 1742 at the behest of Chiara Pisani, the rooms were decorated in accordance with the then-dominant rocaille style. This remarkable decorative explosion culminates in the pòrtego, which is sumptuous with polychrome stuccoes and frescoes by Jacopo Guarana, and where huge Murano chandeliers still glitter with candlelight. Other fine eighteenth-century artists have left their marks in this building amidst the splendor of the furnishings and the objets-d'art: from Giuseppi Angeli to Antonio Zanchi, and even the great Tiepolo, who completed an encomiastic fresco on the ceiling of the red salone, or great hall: The Apotheosis of the Admiral Vettor Pisani (following pages). Sadly, the greatest art treasures housed in this home—two canvases titled Story of Darius, by Veronese and Piazzetta, and Daedalus and Icarus, a youthful masterpiece by Antonio Canova—were moved to other sites during the nineteenth century.

Palazzo Giustinian

This palazzo, consisting of two separate buildings, was erected in the mid-fifteenth century by the Giustinian family, who probably employed Giovanni and Bartolomeo Bon. With its refined late-Gothic design, the facade is punctuated with pointed-arch windows, and is yet another of many influences in the construction of Palazzo Ducale and the Ca' d'Oro. Richard Wagner lived in this building for a number of months, and in 1858 composed the second act of Tristan und Isolde.

"This is not the Mother of God"—exclaimed the composer before Titian's Assunta, or Our Lady of the Assumption—"but Isolde, in her loving transfiguration." Venice and its artistic heritage served as a continual source of inspiration to Wagner, and it was here that he died in 1883. Venice gave him a magnificent burial, which is recounted in Gabriele D'Annunzio's Il Fuoco.

Palazzo Loredan dell'Ambasciatore

The designation "of the Ambassador" is a reminder that, after housing the Marshall Johann Matthias Schulemburg, the valiant defender of Corfu against the Ottoman onslaught, this palazzo for many years housed the embassy of the Austrian Empire. In 1754 the Doge Francesco Loredan ceded it in rental to Filippo di Rosemberg Orsini, the Austrian diplomatic envoy to the Serenissima, for a lease of twenty-nine years, with the understanding that the entire amount of the rent should be paid in advance, and that the embassy should undertake the expense of restoring the palazzo.

Ca' Loredan, built in the second half of the fifteenth century, in the flamboyant late-Gothic style, already presents proto-Renaissance elements such as the marble fascia and the two niches with shield-bearing pages. The morphology of the palazzo is, at any rate, distinctly Gothic, ranging from the four-section window on the piano nobile enriched by large four-lobe elements, to the pendentives of the ogee arches with slender columns with foliate capitals, all the way down to the denticulate panels that frame the window apertures.

Palazzo Priuli all'Osmarin

Built at the end of the fourteenth century and enlarged at the turn of the fifteenth century, this palazzo rises proudly at the intersection of the Rio di San Severo and the Rio dell'Osmarin. The late-Gothic main facade was once adorned with frescoes by Jacopo Palma the Elder. Rare and distinctive in this building are the balconied twin windows at the corners. The one with refined fretwork on the water-bound corner of the building certainly influenced the pergolas of the Ca' d'Oro, built in 1421.

Palazzo van Axel

This palazzo, an important example of late-Gothic architecture, was built between 1473 and 1479 on the site of an existing Veneto-Byzantine building and still preserves that building's decorative elements: paterae and decorative panels on the interior, and the cornice on the second floor. The two facades overlooking the Rio de la Panada and the Rio di San Cancian feature two large Gothic four-section windows, while the pointed-arch portal opening onto the Fondamenta Sanudo is adorned with a denticulate cornice and culminates in a pinnacle with a sculpted relief; note the original wooden doors from the fifteenth century. From 1627 on the palazzo was the property of the van Axels, the family of Flemish merchants who bought into the Venetian aristocracy in 1665. At the turn of the twentieth century the palazzo was purchased by the Counts of Barozzi, who radically restored it. The courtyard staircase and the ground floor portico still show fragments of frescoes, and the well head is an authentic seal on this entirely fifteenth-century setting.

123

Palazzo Centani

This late-Gothic palazzetto, like its fifteenth-century counterparts, is enclosed by a compact facade devoid of the airy stone fretwork typical of Venetian civil architecture in the early fifteen century. The openings of the inflected arches are marked here by a simple marble bay. The courtyard features a handsome staircase, with two flights above broad and elegant pointed arches. Carlo Goldoni—one of Italy's greatest playwrights, and the bard of the Serenissima in the last years of the Republic—was born in this palazzo in 1707. Since 1952 this has been the site of the Museo Goldoni and the adjoining Instituto di Studi Teatrali (institute of theater studies).

Casa Agnusdio

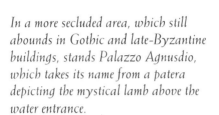

In a more secluded area, which still abounds in Gothic and late-Byzantine buildings, stands Palazzo Agnusdio, which takes its name from a patera depicting the mystical lamb above the water entrance.

This building dates back to the end of the fourteenth century. The facade features a Gothic pentafore, *or five-light window, adorned with fourteenth- to fifteenth-century sculptural reliefs of the symbols of the four Evangelists and the Annunciation. Elegant early-fifteenth-century angels bearing heraldic crests and recycled-Byzantine-style decorative motifs adorn the portal on the land side.*

Church of Sant'Alvise

Built to the indications of St. Louis of Anjou (King Louis IX, Alvise in Venetian dialect), who appeared in a dream to the church's founder Antonia Venier in 1383, more than a century after St. Louis's death, this church was constructed between the fourteenth century and the first years of the fifteenth century. The simple Gothic brick facade marked by six pilaster strips is adorned with small ogee arches beneath its shed-roof eaves. A small rose window interrupts the compact facade directly above the portal, which has a small porch set on tortile columns and adorned with elongated spires. The interior underwent renovations and restorations, especially during the seventeenth and eighteenth centuries when the side altars were built and the flat ceiling was installed—"opened" by fantastic views and architectural trompe l'oeil, a baroque creation of Pietro Ricchi and Antonio Torri. Among the paintings that hang in the church, there are three masterpieces by Tiepolo from the 1740s: the Crown of Thorns, the Flagellation, and the Climb up to Calvary, showing a theatrical use of shading. Also on the walls are a canvas signed Heredes Pauli Caliari (meaning Heir to Paolo Veronese), and small tempera panels from the early fifteenth century with Bible scenes by an artist in the milieu of Lazzaro Bastiani.

Church of San Zanipolo (Santi Giovanni e Paolo, or Saints John and Paul)

This house of worship was built by the Dominican Order in a project that lasted for roughly two centuries; the church has five apses, and was not completed until 1430. The immense Gothic facade (similar to those of other religious buildings erected by the Dominican order, and especially the Florentine church of Santa Maria Novella) balances a pointed-arch upward thrust against the heavy horizontal row of arches cut into its lower order. These elongated arches are actually niches containing sarcophagi. The portal was the work of Bartolomeo Bon and other stonecutters, and was completed between 1459 and 1464 with reused materials taken from Torcello. Complying with a Cistercian design, the intricate plan has apsidal chapels set in a row along the transept. It is over one hundred meters (305 feet) in length, and the dizzying vertical thrust of the cyclopean central aisle is truly astonishing. The cross-vaults high above are supported by tall columns linked by wooden tie-beams. Together with the church of the Frari, this enormous buildings constitutes a sort of Pantheon of the Venetian Republic.

The funerary monument to Pietro Mocenigo (opposite), dated 1476, is the masterpiece of Pietro Lombardo, one of the most noted sculptors and architects of the Venetian Renaissance. Although it has undergone some restoration, the magnificent stained glass is one of the most important artworks ever to emerge from the furnaces of Murano. Designed by Gerolamo Mocetto, it was executed by the master glassmaker Giannantonio Licinio da Lodi between 1510 and 1515.

The public and celebratory nature of the church is emphasized in the Cappella del Rosario (right), a chapel named for a feast in honor of the Virgin Mary and established after the Christian victory over the Turkish fleet at Lepanto. Renovated by Alessandro Vittoria, this chapel holds the remains of Marcantonio Bragadin, the hero of Venetian resistance in the face of the Ottoman forces at Famagusta. Set in the late-mannerist gilded splendor of the wooden ceiling are three paintings by Paolo Veronese and assistants, brought here from the suppressed church of the Umiltà alle Zattere. The Adoration of the Shepherds and the Annunciation together flank the great central panel with the Assumption of the Virgin Mary, an apotheosis that concluded the earthly existence of the Madonna. The Glory of Saint Dominic (opposite) by Giovanni Battista Piazzetta between 1725 and 1727 emphasizes his skill in giving a sense of material while creating brilliant and suffusive chiaroscuro effects, anticipating the work of Tiepolo. In 1542, late in his career, Lorenzo Lotto painted for this church the Charity of Saint Anthony (page 132), which takes its distance from the colorism of Titian and the heroic, transfigured depictions of the sacred typical of Paolo Veronese and Jacopo Tintoretto. Among the numerous artworks, note the Renaissance Polyptych of Saint Vincent Ferrer (page 133), a youthful creation of Giovanni Bellini (1465).

130

Much like the church of San Zanipolo, this church houses the remains of many illustrious figures, among them several renowned artists. The tripartite facade of this, the largest church in Venice, features a large rose window flanked by two smaller rose windows over the side aisles. It is distinguished by a linear and majestic Gothic style. The interior of this church is one immense brick volume built by the Franciscan Order beginning in the thirteenth century, and is unique for its masterpieces of Renaissance art. Beneath the ribs of the Gothic vaults, powerful wooden tie-beams link together the twelve stout pylons that split the great hall into a nave and two aisles.

The wooden choir by Marco Cozzi, built in 1468, also clearly marks the transition from Gothic to Renaissance. A lavish creation with intarsias and gilt woodcarvings, it is divided into three orders with 124 stalls (detail opposite). The face of the choir is a marble curtain wall, which was a joint effort of the Bon workshop and the Lombardo masters, and is the only choir in Venice that has been left in the center of the nave, where it was originally placed.

The monument to Antonio Canova (d. 1822) was designed by the sculptor himself, and was executed by his pupils in 1827. Built in a pure neoclassical style, it houses Canova's heart in a porphyry vase, while the rest of his body lies in the church that he designed in Possagno, where he was born. The mausoleum (opposite) of Tiziano Vecellio, or Titian, was built at the behest of Luigi and Pietro Zandomeneghi between 1838 and 1852.

The remarkable novelty of the Pesaro altarpiece painted by Titian between 1519 and 1526 lies in the sharp break with the idea of a central, axial principle of composition. Instead, the painting is composed at a sharply diagonal angle emphasized by the throne, the massive columns in the background, and the three separate groups of figures. Also by Titian, the Assumption (1516–1518) (opposite) is a masterpiece of color and dynamic shapes.

Donatello's St. John the Baptist (opposite), dated 1450 and originally intended for the altar of the Cappella dei Fiorentini, features stylistic elements that are perhaps more typical of late-Gothic art; nonetheless it placed the sculptor among the most important figures of the early Renaissance. Also preserved in this church is an altarpiece by Giovanni Bellini (1488), depicting the Virgin Mary with the Christ Child and putti playing musical instruments, with four saints. The dramatic naturalism of the work makes Bellini a patriarch of the Venetian Renaissance, who with such foreign influences as Albrecht Dürer blazed a trail in the early sixteenth century for a new generation of local painters.

139

Church of the Madonna dell'Orto

This church, formerly dedicated to Saint Christopher, became a sanctuary of the Virgin Mary in 1377 when a statue of the Virgin that had once stood in a nearby garden patch was moved into the church. The statue attracted the faithful with its reputation for working miracles. Construction ensued, and continued throughout the fifteenth century; the tripartite facade corresponding to the interior plan can be compared to its colossal counterparts in the churches of the Frari and San Zanipolo. Numerous works by Tintoretto—who lived nearby and was deeply bound to this house of worship—include two colossal paintings in the pentagonal apsidal chapel. The church also holds a lovely small Madonna by Giovanni Bellini, and a Renaissance altarpiece by Giambattista Cima da Conegliano, titled John the Baptist among Saints Peter, Mark, Jerome, and Paul (opposite). The late-fifteenth-century portal in the center of the facade exemplifies the transition from the pointed-arch vernacular of the latest phase of Gothic seen in its exterior arch—whose extrados features phytomorphic ornaments—to the Renaissance, as represented by the interior, round-headed arch with Corinthian side-columns.

140

Church of San Giovanni in Bragora

In the dense curtain of buildings that surrounds the Campo Bandiera e Moro stands the church of San Giovanni in Bragora. The tripartite brick facade, built in 1475, is marked by a late-Gothic style, which was already obsolete by the time the roof was built—note how the large central arch links to two curvilinear side elements, a clear forerunner of certain creations of Mauro Codussi. The apse, completed by the Ticinese artist Sebastiano Mariani between 1480 and 1495, is a thoroughly Renaissance construction. The interior is cozy and appealing, with its nave and two aisles set on a basilican plan, with a wooden, ship's-keel ceiling in the late-Gothic style. There are numerous artworks: paintings by Jacopo Palma the Younger, Alvise and Bartolomeo Vivarini, Paris Bordone, Jacopo Marieschi, Francesco Bissolo, and Francesco Maggiotto. High on the main altar is the Baptism of Christ (opposite) by Cima da Conegliano, who also painted Constantine Holding the Cross and Saint Helena for this church. The hovering, distant atmosphere, and the figures with traces of the Gothic style, set against a Venetian landscape, pale blue and neo-Platonic, make this an exquisite masterpiece of the Renaissance.

Abbey of San Gregorio

This Benedictine abbey—founded in the ninth century by the monks of Sant'Ilario, a powerful religious community and a major political and religious center in the early years of the Republic—was rebuilt in the pointed-arch style in the mid-fifteenth century. Suppressed as a convent in 1775, in 1806 it was also eliminated as a parish church. The Gothic church of this complex, which now houses a respected restoration workshop, was nationalized and stripped of the important artworks that adorned it. The tripartite facade, on the other hand, is still intact, and features a handsome portal and a rose window. After 1461 the polygonal apse was built, its vertical structure reinforced by its elegant windows. In what was the residential building of the monks, there is a square colonnaded cloister that dates from 1342, while the facade—adorned with trilobate windows and a flower-motif portal crowned by an exquisite Gothic relief—overlooks the Grand Canal and the Salute.

Abbey of the Misericordia

Set on the Campo dell'Abbazia, a silent location well off the beaten track, is the monumental complex of the Misericordia. First founded as early as A.D. 936, the church was originally named Santa Maria di Valverde; it presents a baroque-style facade crowned by a curvilinear central pediment, adorned with sculptures and reliefs. The Gothic structure, which replaced the earlier Byzantine structure in the thirteenth century, was then once again rebuilt between 1651 and 1659 by the Bolognese architect Clemente Moli, at the behest of Senatore Gaspare Moro, whose family were patrons of the abbey from 1348 on. Moli was a follower of Bernini, and often worked with Baldassarre Longhena as a sculptor. The Scuola Vecchia della Misericordia—the original head-quarters of the religious organization of the Misericordia, documented as far back as 1261—is connected to the church by a little Gothic cloister, a relic of the suppressed monastery. Completed in 1451, the structure (possibly designed by someone in the milieu of Bon) has a lovely Gothic facade surmounted by a mixed-style crown, flanked by two tall aedicules. The symmetrical pointed-arch windows once framed a splendid bas-relief by Bartolomeo Bon that adorned the central portal—it was removed in 1612 and is now in the Victoria and Albert Museum in London. Originating at the side portal on the water is a public, porticoed walkway completed in 1508, that animates the water facade with its regular frames.

Church of Santo Stefano

Appertaining to the Augustinian convent complex, this church was the result of the reconstruction of a thirteenth-century structure, beginning around 1350 and completed early in the fifteenth century. The tripartite brick facade is enriched by a flamboyant Gothic portal executed by Bartolomeo Bon. The interior has a ship's-keel ceiling featuring five lobed coffers with rose motifs in a honeycomb pattern, an exquisite piece of Venetian cabinetry done in the early fifteenth century. Funerary monuments of various periods and styles surround the tomb of the Doge Francesco Morosini, which has pride of place in the nave. Sculptures from the workshop of the Lombardo family, and by Alessandro Vittoria, Gerolamo Campagna, and Giulio del Moro, along with paintings by Michele Marieschi, Leonardo Corona, and Nicolò Bambini adorn the altars. The Gothic choir loft of the monks, with inlaid and carved stalls, dates from 1488—the work of Marco Cozzi and Leonardo Scalamanzio—and once stood in the center of the nave. In the sacristy are paintings by Paris Bordone, Jacopo Palma the Elder, and Sante Peranda; and over an early-sixteenth-century altar frontal there are three impressively vigorous canvases from Tintoretto's prime, The Last Supper (page 151), The Washing of the Feet, and Christ in the Garden. Also preserved here is a canvas by Vittore Carpaccio (once housed in the nearby church of San Vidal): San Vitale on Horseback (page 150). Also worthy of note is a very fine relief by Antonio Canova (1801), the funerary stele of Senatore Giovanni Falier (this page).

150

The "modern" city
and the renaissance period

Mauro Codussi,
Palazzo Vendramin Calergi.

Arsenale

Once the heart of the military and mercantile might of the Venetian Republic, the Arsenale still occupies a vast area. Although there is no reliable basis for the date of 1104 that is traditionally offered for the foundation of the Arsenale, it is certain that an area used for the storage, repair, and construction of galleys, weapons, rigging, and oars did exist in the early years of the thirteenth century. The Arsenale grew progressively in importance throughout the fifteenth and sixteenth centuries, at one point employing more than sixteen thousand workers, and stretching across the entire northeastern section of the city. The entrance gate to the Arsenale was built during the rule of Doge Pasquale Malipiero to resemble a triumphal arch honoring the maritime glory of the Republic. Work on it began in 1460, and the design incorporates the new classical motifs. Standing out proudly above the jutting trabeation (which rests upon eleventh-century Veneto-Byzantine capitals taken from a prior structure) is the winged lion of St. Mark, symbol of Venice, set in an aedicule topped by a tympanum. The two lions immediately on either side of the gate originally came from Athens, and were part of the plunder brought back to Venice by Francesco Morosini following his reconquest of Morea (the Peloponnesus) in 1687. The other two lions reached Venice earlier. The central lion to the right of the gate is a Greek sculpture dating from the sixth century B.C. (its head is more recent), originally from the island of Delos. It commemorates of the reconquest of Corfu in 1716.

Palazzo Dario

A civic devotion pervaded the early Renaissance period in Venice, striving to glorify the city, and leaving to funerary monuments the task of exalting the virtues of individuals and the pride of aristocratic dynasties. This building was erected between 1487 and 1492 under the supervision of an artist from the milieu of the Lombardo family, and possibly by Pietro Lombardo himself, at the behest of Giovanni Dario, secretary of the Venetian legation to the court of the Ottoman emperor Mehmet II.

The building features elements of local tradition such as its asymmetrical facade and the polychrome marble, which contrast with such Renaissance features as the classical decorations of the facade and the shape of the arches. The facade overlooking the garden, on the other hand, preserves the late-Gothic style of the previous construction, which dated from the fourteenth or fifteenth century.

Fondaco dei Tedeschi

There was always a sizable Germanic colony living in Venice. While the city may have been considered the gateway to the East, nonetheless its geographical proximity to the German regions made it a major stop-over point for travelers from the north. This building, given to the Germans as their national headquarters in the city, stood in Rialto, the economic center of town. When the building was destroyed by fire in 1505, the Venetian Senate, aware of its commercial importance, entrusted its reconstruction to Giorgio Spavento, who designed a massive square building, larger and more comfortable than its predecessor, wrapped around an interior courtyard and marked by several orders of airy loggias. Spavento died in 1509 and was replaced as the director of construction by Antonio Scarpagnino. The elevation overlooking the Grand Canal, its center emblazoned with a five-arch portico, is marked on either side by stone pilasters that indicate two separate structural bodies, which were originally higher at the center. The height of the facade was made uniform during the restoration of 1836; at that time the entire line of the eaves was adorned with pinnacles made of Istrian stone. In 1508 Giorgione was commissioned to fresco the main facade and the right side elevation, visible from the Ponte di Rialto. Working with Giorgione was the young Titian. The building's three stories were covered by the work of the two artists in a fresco that featured nudes. Fragments of it, as well as a single whole figure, are now in the Ca' d'Oro.

This church was begun in 1450 under Antonio Gambello, and then carried on by Pietro Lombardo. It is an example of contamination between an extreme Gothic style and the new architectural language of the humanists. The stylistic duality of this house of worship is expressed powerfully in the contrast between the simple brick facade and the refined relief work of the Lombardesque portal, as well as the contrast between the rigor of the central aisle and the spatial contrivances of the presbytery, which is entered through a triumphal arch built by the workshop of Pietro Lombardo. Three of the greatest artworks that were once housed here—the Prayer in the Garden by Marco Basaiti, an altarpiece by Giovanni Bellini, and the Presentation of Jesus in the Temple by Vittore Carpaccio—were taken to the Gallerie dell'Accademia following the religious suppressions under Napoleon. This church still boasts a noteworthy collection of art, however, including a Nativity by Gerolamo Savoldo (1540), and considerable Tuscan influences ranging from the Lucchese clients for the Martini chapel, for which Antonio Rossellino executed the altar with a marble altarpiece dedicated to St. John the Baptist, to the majolica Della Robbia ceiling.

163

This Gothic building dates back to the fifteenth century, and takes its name from a relief depicting a man walking in front of a camel, which is set in the wall of the facade to the right of the second-story balcony. This figure is traditionally said to represent the earliest owners of the building, of Levantine provenance. Note the fragments of friezes and Byzantine paterae in the masonry; the left corner window on the second floor features a fragment of a Roman altar, used as a column. The central pointed-arch loggia on the upper story once again shows the architectural language developed in the Ca' d'Oro, mingled with Eastern influences and tending toward a fuller and more "fleshy" interpretation of the ethereal style of Venetian Gothic.

Scala Contarini del Bovolo

Set on the landward side of a palazzo that incorporates features of the Gothic and proto-Renaissance styles rises the celebrated Scala del Bovolo—a Venetianism meaning "spiral staircase," which so profoundly struck the imagination of the populace of Venice that in time the term was used to describe not only the building as a whole but also the family that owned it. Built in 1499 at the behest of the aristocrat Pietro Contarini, probably under the supervision of the master builder Giovanni Candi, the spiral staircase is contained in a tower with a circular plan, after the Byzantine archetype. The length of the staircase is punctuated by buttress arches, light-hearted architectural solutions of the Veneto-Byzantine tradition that seek to fit in with the five stacked orders of the loggia.

Palazzo Corner Spinelli

This palazzo was designed by Mauro Codussi in 1490, and features an elevation in which a double order of windows sits on the high rusticated base, clearly influenced by the style of the central Italian Renaissance. The twin-light windows crowned by a blind oculus constitute a special combination of local late-Gothic styles with new elements of humanist architecture, marked by a round-arch ribbing in accordance with the aesthetics of Codussi. The interior, renovated by Michele Sanmicheli, was the site in 1542 of the first appearance of Mannerism in Venice, with the work of Giorgio Vasari, who designed and executed a ceiling with perspectival panels, painted with daringly foreshortened figures. This work changed the course of Venetian painting, and influenced a new generation of painters, especially Veronese and Tintoretto, as well as the great Titian. The panels were later broken up and are now in various collections. The coffered ceiling that we now see also dates from the sixteenth century (1547, to be precise) and features an intricate carved decoration of gold against dark blue. Each of the square bays of the ceiling, set off by a pronounced cornice, displays a different decorative motif: eagles, minute panoplies, paterae, masks, phytomorphic elements, and urns wind around the circular pine cones that occupy the center of each panel.

Palazzo Grimani

This building is a proud expression of that section of the Venetian aristocracy of the sixteenth century that, in its building programs, also sought to glorify the gens, or extended family—in this case, the Grimani, a family with close ties to the papal Curia. Construction was begun by the Veronese architect Michele Sanmicheli in 1550 and then carried on, following his death in 1559, by Guglielmo de' Grigi, who completed it two years later. The monumental façade is split into three parts in the traditional manner by massive horizontal fascias, and punctuated by a series of Serlian windows. On the ground floor there is a deep, triumphal colonnaded atrium with three open arches clearly borrowed from ancient Roman models. The floor plan is the result of an adaptation of the layout used previously for Ca' Corner de la Ca' Granda, with a trapezoidal lot that is difficult to resolve in architectural terms.

Palazzo dei Camerlenghi

Dominating the Grand Canal, isolated from the surrounding buildings and well exposed from every angle, this palazzo has no main facade; this factor is the source of the remarkably lush decoration that can be found on every elevation. Built by Antonio Scarpagnino between 1525 and 1528, the building stands as the conclusion of the renovation of the entire adjoining Rialto area following the great fire of 1514. The white structure of Istrian stone served three functions: prison, mercantile loggia, and headquarters of the treasurers of the Serenissima Repubblica. The outer walls were originally adorned with polychrome stone decorations, now lost, that stood out against the white stone facing. The palazzo has an herbarium behind it, closed in by the bulk of the Fabbriche Vecchie. The building now houses the Corte dei Conti, an Italian administrative court.

Palazzo Vendramin Calergi

This building is a true exemplar of the Venetian vernacular juxtaposed with Tuscan elements of Renaissance conception. A re-elaboration of plans previously used in Palazzo Corner Spinelli, the palazzo was built by Mauro Codussi between 1481 and 1504. It was the Lombardo family, however, that completed it in 1509, while Vincenzo Scamozzi added the wing overlooking the garden in the early seventeenth century. The facade, with its inscription non nobis domine, as if to beg forgiveness for having used the building as a lavish aristocratic residence, features a double sequence of distinctive twin-light windows, punctuated by twin columns (single columns in the center) compressed above and below by jutting courses. The massive cornice, decorated with heraldic motifs, is a clear echo of the style of central Italian humanism. The palazzo has a number of rooms—including one upholstered in gilded sixteenth-century leather—with spectacular fireplaces and Mannerist decorations. Other halls were modernized in 1844 by the Duchesse de Berry. The palazzo is now the winter site of the Venice Casino.

169

Ca' Corner de la Ca' Granda

Giorgio Corner, a member of one of Venice's most powerful families and the brother of the queen of Cyprus, purchased a Byzantine-Gothic building from Bartolomeo Malombra, with an ambitious architectural program in mind, which was left unfinished at his death in 1527. It was Giorgio's nephew Zorzetto who entrusted the job to Jacopo Sansovino, thus ensuring that this building became the first manifestation in the lagoon territory of the new res aedificatoria. Completed around 1560, the palazzo loudly proclaims this aristocratic pride with an elevation set upon a rusticated Vitruvian atrium with three open arches. This is an authentic monument glorifying the gens, with a floor plan that is organized in an innovative manner around a square "Roman-style" courtyard influenced by the ideological tenets of the Renaissance. It was purchased by the city during Austrian rule, and since 1866 has housed the city prefecture.

Palazzo Trevisan on Murano

Between the fifteenth and sixteenth centuries, the island of Murano became a choice holiday spot for Venetian aristocrats, an ideal setting for the leisure time of patrician men of letters. Palazzo Trevisan, a sophisticated late-Renaissance building designed and erected by an unknown architect in 1557, is emblematic of the intellectual alliance—comprising among others Alessandro Vittoria, Paolo Veronese, and Andrea Palladio—who would gather on this island to speak and discuss under the patronage of Daniele Barbaro. The abstract façade, comprised of modules that once framed the now-lost frescoes of Prospero Bresciano, is dominated by an immense central Serlian window and by the dramatically jutting cornice. Inside there is a remarkable decorative program of refined stuccoes by Vittoria, grotesques and Arcadian landscapes by Bernardino India, and above all, a series of frescoes done in 1557 by Paolo Veronese, clear forerunners of the frescoes in Villa Barbaro a Maser.

Church of Santa Maria dei Miracoli

This church was built by Pietro Lombardo between 1481—the year in which the decision was made to undertake its construction on the site where Francesco Amadi had placed a greatly venerated altarpiece of the Virgin Mary—and 1494. Conceived in simple geometric forms—a parallelepiped structure and a cylinder with a cupola—Santa Maria dei Miracoli is faced both outside and inside with polychrome marble broken here and there by disks and panels of porphyry invoking the origins of the Serenissima, but revised with proto-Renaissance elegance by the workshop of the Lombardo family. The single aisle of the interior is set apart from the main chapel, which is raised on a platform to dominate the interior of the church. Here hangs a Gothic panel of the Madonna with Child, standing out against a high-medieval flowered field. Extending before the hall is the hanging choir loft, and on the wooden ceiling are paintings from the milieu of Titian. In the gold coffers of the magnificent barrel vault, one can hardly miss the fifty figures of prophets and patriarchs painted toward the end of the fifteenth century by Piermaria and Gerolamo Pennacchi, Vincenzo Dalle Destre, and Lattanzio da Rimini. The marble balustrades on each side of the main chapel are worked in a refined decorative manner, with four smaller sculptures on the dominant corners. The artwork, like the entire conception of this house of worship, is of Lombardesque origin, belonging to a school that strained to achieve a sort of resuscitation of the Veneto-Byzantine vernacular in the light of the new ideas of Tuscan humanism.

Church of San Giorgio dei Greci

The Greek community, present in the city of Venice from the eleventh century on, swelled greatly in numbers following the end of the Eastern Empire in 1453, with the capture of Constantinople by the Ottoman army. It was not until 1526, however, that the Greeks obtained from the Venetian Senate the authorization to practice the Orthodox religion, and to build their own church. Construction of the building was begun in 1539 by Sante Lombardo and was continued by Giannantonio Chiona. The church stands free on the courtyard overlooking the water, protected by buildings of the community. At the sides of the church stand the late-sixteenth-century campanile by Simone Sorella and two baroque buildings erected within a magnificent enclosure by Baldassarre Longhena between 1678 and 1680. In them are found the Scuola di San Nicolò and the Collegio Flangini, which hosts Greek cultural institutions.

The interior of the church features a single nave, ending in the magnificent iconostasis, behind which is concealed the presbytery, reserved for the officiants. The iconostasis is decorated with impressive figures of saints and the Twelve Feasts against a golden surface, dating back to the sixteenth century by the Cretan artist Michael Damaskinos. Giovanni da Cipro, Emmanuel Zane, Giorgio Klonzas—all members of the artistic school of Candia that dared to disturb the centuries-old fixity of Byzantine art with the innovative styles of Venetian art—worked here together at the end of the sixteenth century. This school followed in the wake of the last Titianesque colorism, and from its midst emerged the visionary genius Domenico Theotokopulos, known as El Greco.

Church of San Giovanni Crisostomo

The understated plaster facade crowned by the distinctive curvilinear features of Mauro Codussi's architectural style corresponds to the simple, intellectual harmony of the interior, built to a Greek-cross plan and surmounted by a cupola that communicates a powerful upward thrust. The church was rebuilt by Codussi between 1497 and 1504, and presents many of the same devices used five years previously in the church of Santa Maria Formosa, in which the gray architraves set off against the plaster create a remarkable chiaroscuro effect, while the capitals that support the light vault create an elegant visual detail. Belonging to the same stylistic milieu, striving to mingle local tradition with Renaissance innovations, is the Lombardesque marble altarpiece from the early sixteenth century, depicting the Coronation of the Virgin (opposite) with refined relief-work and exquisite perspective and rich in archaic features, especially the Gothic-style hair of the Madonna. There are two masterpieces in this church. One is the altarpiece of St. Jerome, St. Christopher, and St. Augustine; one of the last works of Giovanni Bellini, it is infused with the revolutionary approach to color of the young Titian. The second is Sebastiano del Piombo's altarpiece of St. John Chrysostome, St. Paul, St. John the Baptist, St. Liberal, St. Magdalene, St. Cecilia, and St. Catherine, painted between 1508 and 1509 with a daring metaphysical use of color that is clearly a forerunner of Mannerism.

TVLLII LOMBARDI OPVS

177

Church of Santa Maria Mater Domini

One of the first authentic Renaissance buildings to be erected in the lagoon territory, this church was built between 1504 and 1540 in a simple, elegant style echoing the work of Codussi. It is believed that the church was designed by Giovanni Buora and Jacopo Sansovino, who supposedly completed the façade. The interior, built to a Greek-cross plan, is remarkably luminous, given the cramped location of the building. The design shows a classic Venetian proto-Renaissance conception, emphasizing a compromise between elements from the local tradition, such as the Byzantine cupola, and other, central Italian inspirations. In the nave, punctuated by towering pillars and broad stone fascias contrasting with the white plaster, the Renaissance is evident in the Lombardesque carved stone altars, the sculptures by Lorenzo Bregno, paintings by Jacopo Tintoretto and Bonifacio de' Pitati, and a relief in colored stucco from the milieu of Donatello above the main altar, itself a further reference to Tuscan humanism. Still, the masterpiece of this church is undoubtedly the painting of the Martyrdom of St. Christine (opposite) by Vincenzo Catena (1520). The gentle, luminous Venetian landscape and the influence of Bellini are crystallized by the sophisticated array of colors, and the sweep of the figures' silhouettes in a visual language showing northern and proto-Mannerist influences.

179

Already in existence as early as the seventh century, this church was rebuilt in the ninth century and transformed into its present form by Mauro Codussi in 1492. Simple, exceedingly pure volumes rise from a Latin-cross floor plan. The interplay of vaults and arches, emphasized by ribs that stand out against the white plaster, shows the direct inspiration of central Italian architectural masterpieces, though clearly that influence is layered onto structural elements deeply rooted in the local vernacular. The triptych by Bartolomeo Vivarini titled **Virgin Mary of Mercy** dates back to 1473, and is set in an elegant carved stone altar.

The outer elevations of the church, which dominate the square, culminate in a barn-facade elevation overlooking the water, built in 1542 and dominated by a monument to Vincenzo Cappello, whose family underwrote the costs of construction. The other facades date back to 1604, and still bear heraldic crests and busts of the Cappello family. Also dating from the seventeenth century is the bell tower by Francesco Zucconi, which is entered by a door beneath a grotesque mask meant to ward off evil.

Church of San Michele in Isola

This convent church of the Camaldoli monks dates back to the tenth century, but was completely rebuilt between 1469 and 1478 by Mauro Codussi, the pioneer in Venice of the humanistic architectural revolution that was already dominant in central Italy. The white mass of the tripartite façade in Istrian stone, topped by an elegant semicircular tympanum and two buttresses with refined reliefs framing the central oculus, makes this the first truly Renaissance religious building on the lagoon, establishing a prototype that was to spread through the Venetian dominions. Alongside the main elevation is the exquisite hexagonal structure of the Cappella Emiliani, built in 1530 by Guglielmo de' Grigi, known as Bergamasco. On the other side is the fifteenth-century cloister that constitutes the entrance to the town cemetery set here in the nineteenth century, following the unification of the islands of San Cristoforo and San Michele.

This church, which traces its earliest foundation to the seventh century, was rebuilt repeatedly over the centuries, until the sixteenth century, when it was finally given the appearance we see today. Giorgio Spavento, the architect who first designed this final version, was replaced in time by Tullio Lombardo, but it was Jacopo Sansovino who completed construction on this, one of the most intricate and complex construction projects in the history of Venetian building. The main elevation was built in 1663 by Giuseppe Sardi, and is adorned with sculptures by Bernardo Falcone. The solemn Renaissance interior, with a lavish floor of marble intarsia-work, is flooded with light that pours down through three lanterns added to the cupolas by Vincenzo Scamozzi in 1569. Sculptures by Alessandro Vittoria and Gerolamo Campagna, paintings by Jacopo Palma the Younger, the altarpiece of Saint Leonardo and Saint Lorenzo Giustiniani e Santi by Francesco Fontebasso, and an organ designed by Sansovino with shutters painted by Francesco Vecellio—brother of the celebrated Titian—all adorn this church. Buried here are Caterina Cornaro, Queen of Cyprus, and in another funerary monument designed by Jacopo Sansovino, the Doge Francesco Venier (opposite). The outstanding artistic treasures of this church, however, are two canvases by Titian: a Transfiguration (page 186) on the main altar, a powerful and bold creation of the artist's maturity, and an Annunciation (page 187) dating to 1560–66, with a glittering, spiraling, liquid and golden light, set in the Cappella Cornovì.

185

187

The facade of this church is permeated with the classical style, built to a design by Antonio Scarpagnino from 1505 to 1548. The interior is built on a Latin-cross plan with a single nave with a presbytery topped by a cupola, and is further articulated by the hanging choir loft that extends along the sides. The details of the actual architecture mingle with the spectacular trompe-l'oeil architecture produced by Veronese's masterful painting. Paolo Veronese—buried in this church at the base of the organ whose doors he decorated in 1559— was deeply linked to the order of the Gerolamini, and was a titular of the church and of the adjoining convent. Between 1551 and 1565 he painted several of his masterpieces here, frescoes and canvases that comprise an artistic complex of unrivaled magnificence. In the Cappella Lando, to the left of the main chapel, there is a glazed terra-cotta floor dating from 1510, at the center of which is emblazoned the crest of the patrons, a family that produced a doge of the Republic in the sixteenth century. The tiles depict masks, tiny landscapes, panoplies, allegorical motifs, and images of animals quite similar to those found in the Belgian abbey of Herckenrode, which is also the work of a Venetian workshop. The artist clearly had little experience in decorating tiles, and used drawings with a circular structure for this unfamiliar geometric medium, shapes more suitable for the decoration of dishes or bowls.

Church of San Zaccaria

Founded in the ninth century, the building features a proto-Renaissance facade that shows late-Gothic forms with a strong vertical flavor. The enormous structure that we see today is the result of two different phases of construction between 1444 and 1500: a late-Gothic project supervised by Antonio Gambello, and a Renaissance intervention by Mauro Codussi. Gambello designed and built both the Cappella di Sant'Atanasio and the Cappella di San Tarasio, a structure done in the Gothic style dating back to the first half of the fifteenth century. Codussi worked on the main facade, which he developed in a series of orders of different widths, crowned by curvilinear forms. The church features a floor plan with three aisles separated by tall columns, and contains one of the most remarkable bodies of artwork to be found in the city of Venice: from capitals by Antonio Buora to masterpieces by Giovanni Bellini and Antonio Vivarini. The wooden choir of the Cappella di Sant'Atanasio by the brothers Marco and Francesco Cozzi was altered at the end of the sixteenth century. The altarpiece, by Jacopo Tintoretto, depicts the Birth of St. John. The Cappella di San Tarasio preserves at the foot of the altar the remains of a mosaic that once adorned the apse of a prior Byzantine-Romanesque church dating from the twelfth century.

The artistic format of the polyptych, which was introduced into the lagoon territory by Paolo Veneziano, is represented here in its more canonical form by Antonio Vivarini in his Madonna di Mastro Stefano (1443, below), with the painting enriched by the background of gilded wood.

In 1505, at the age of seventy-five, Giovanni Bellini completed a masterpiece for the church that strives to resolve the relationship between light and color. This altarpiece of St. Zachary (opposite) was carried off in 1797 at the orders of Napoleon, and was returned from Paris in 1816.

The funerary monument with a bust of Alessandro Vittoria at its center (opposite) was begun by the artist himself in 1556, and continued by his brother-in-law and closest collaborator Alessandro Rubini. Upon Rubini's death, the cenotaph was completed by his followers.

ALEXANDER · VICTORIA
QVI · VIVENS · VIVOS · DVXIT
E · MARMORE · VVLTVS

On this island—which may have been inhabited even as early as Roman times—a Benedictine monastery was built in 968; even at its origin, this monastery was similar in importance to Piazza San Marco and its various buildings. Given ever greater wealth and significance by popes and emperors, the monastery was secularized in 1806. Since 1951 the complex has been the headquarters of the Fondazione Giorgio Cini.

The facade of the church is dominated by a triangular pediment set on four Corinthian columns, adjoined by two half pediments marked with pilaster strips. Designed by Andrea Palladio, the church was begun in 1566, and it was completed at the beginning of the seventeenth century by Simone Sorella. The interior is designed according to a Latin-cross plan revolving around a vast, deep choir. Split into a nave and two aisles and topped by a cupola set directly onto the transept, this church boasts numerous fine paintings, including the majestic Last Supper by Jacopo Tintoretto (1594), set on the wall of the presbytery. In the upper chapel are relics of the conclave that elected Pope Pius VII, and the altar features a painting by Vittore Carpaccio, done in 1516.

The cloister was begun by Palladio in 1579, and was unfinished at his death in 1580. A stairway leading from the cloister is the theatrical creation of the unrivaled star of Venetian baroque, Baldassarre Longhena. It is split into two symmetrical flights, and was built between 1641 and 1643. Longhena also rebuilt the library, which was destroyed by fire in 1614, in the style of Michelozzi Michelozzo. This impressive baroque setting houses more than a hundred thousand volumes.

Church of the Zitelle
(Church and hospice of Santa Maria della Visitazione)

This church dedicated to Our Lady of the Visitation forms a single architectural complex with the hospice that surrounds it on three sides. In the eighteenth century this charitable institution housed poor young women who devoted their time to the embroidery of remarkable intricate lace, and to music, as evidenced by the very structure of the hall: square, with snub corners rounded off for considerations of acoustics. The facade has two orders surmounted by a pediment with small bell towers on either side. It was designed by Andrea Palladio, and built two years after his death in 1582 by Jacopo Bozzetto. The building is topped by a vast cupola on slender Corinthian pillars, which enlarge the internal perspective of the church, which was renovated radically in the eighteenth century. The paintings in the church date from the sixteenth century, and include work by Francesco Bassano and by Antonio Vassillachi, as well as Prayer in the Garden by Jacopo Palma the Younger.

Scuola Grande della Misericordia

The stern voice of Alessandro Caravia, a figure well-rooted in the Venetian culture of his time, was distinguished by the new religious zeal of the Reformation. In 1541 he issued from his workshop in Rialto a call for austerity addressed to the major Scuole, which he felt were undertaking excessively ambitious programs of construction, and forgetting their original roles as charitable institutions. The compact brick structure of the Scuola Grande della Misericordia, designed in 1532 and punctuated by large windows, elongated niches, and geometric reliefs, testifies in its incomplete state to the obstacles the Renaissance style encountered in sixteenth-century Venice. Its designer Jacopo Sansovino balked at the rejection of his innovative ideas, and in 1544 abandoned construction of the project.

Built as an offering of thanksgiving following the plague of 1576, this sanctuary was begun by Andrea Palladio in 1577, and ever since its foundation it has been the destination, on the third Sunday in July, of a procession that crosses the Canale della Giudecca over a long bridge built on boats. Completed by Antonio da Ponte in 1592, the structure rises majestically from its rusticated podium among the adjoining buildings, its facade resolved in a harmonious progression of intersecting planes, a geometric counterplay of triangular and rectangular volumes. A monumental staircase reminiscent of the many staircases designed by Palladio for his villas, leads to the arched portal, which is surmounted by a pediment and flanked by two niches with sculptures by Gerolamo Campagna. The interior, with artworks by Alvise Vivarini, Francesco Bassano, Pietro Vecchia, Carlo Saraceni, and Paolo Veronese and his school, is built on a Latin-cross plan. Broad clerestory windows light the single nave flanked by three chapels on each side. In the presbytery, formed of two semicircular apses, there is a main altar with a large baroque tabernacle and bronze sculptures, also by Campagna.

This first project of Jacopo Sansovino in Venice, the church of the Franciscans almost constitutes a manifesto of the advent of the full Renaissance in Venice in the third decade of the sixteenth century. The well balanced Latin-cross floor plan is marked by the neo-Platonic conceptions of the Prior Francesco Zorzi—author of the Problemata, the treatise De Harmonia Mundi, and a determined supporter of a spiritual reformation of the Catholic church—in a complex interplay of proportions based on the number three. The programs of the Gritti palazzo of the family of the doge, which overlooks the square across from the church, are mirrored in the chapels. For instance, the remarkable Cappella dei Giustinian is adorned with sculptures and Lombardesque reliefs all belonging to families linked to the milieu of the doge. Among the artworks by Paolo Veronese, Alessandro Vittoria, Giovanni Bellini, and Giambattista Tiepolo, one should note in particular the Virgin Mary Enthroned with the Christ Child (opposite), painted by Antonio da Negroponte around 1470. Rich in symbolic meaning, it reveals an encounter between humanistic naturalism and a still more determinedly late-Gothic style. After the death of Andrea Gritti in 1538, it was the Grimani family (especially the patriarch Aquileia Giovanni Grimani, who had already commissioned a secular, tributary decoration alla romana on the vault of his chapel) that sponsored work on the church, culminating after 1568 with the erection of the tripartite facade by Andrea Palladio.

201

Church of San Pietro di Castello

The little island of San Pietro di Castello—also known as Olivolo—was one of the earliest settlements in the lagoon area. In early times it was garrisoned to defend the city, but it later became the residence and headquarters of the bishop, originally subject to the episcopal authority of Grado, but elevated to patriarchal status in 1451, when Pope Nicholas V invested Saint Lorenzo Giustiniani with this status. In 1807 when the title was transferred to the Basilica di San Marco, the church was made a city cathedral. Originally based on an idea of Andrea Palladio's, and suggestive of the facade of the Redentore, the rigorous white building of Istrian stone was built by Francesco Smeraldi and construction was continued by an architect influenced by Vincenzo Scamozzi, a certain Giovanni Grapiglia, who completed it in 1621. The main altar is an impressive baroque contrivance that looms over the presbytery. It was built in 1649 by Clemente Moli, who also executed the sculptures to designs by Baldassarre Longhena, while the apsidal vault was frescoed by Giovanni Pellegrini. Longhena also designed the baroque Cappella del Cardinale Vendramin (1663), which is decorated with sculptures by Melchiorre Barthel and an altarpiece by Luca Giordano. To the right of the church stands the bell tower built by Mauro Codussi around 1490 and faced with slabs of Istrian stone. Adjoining the church is the long, simple structure of the Palazzo Patriarcale. The setting seems enveloped in a haze of the past— an impression broken only by the feast of the patron saint, an important occasion for all Venetians, and for the inhabitants of the Sestiere di Castello in particular.

Scuola di San Giorgio degli Schiavoni (Scuola Dalmata dei Santi Giorgio e Trifone)

The Scuola degli Schiavoni was founded by the Dalmatian confraternity and was originally set up in 1451 in the church of San Giovanni dei Cavalieri di Malta. The facade of the Scuola, clearly influenced by Jacopo Sansovino's vernacular, was rebuilt in 1551 upon a more modest late-fifteenth-century structure by Giovanni De Zan, builder of the Arsenale. Carved stone reliefs, including one depicting St. George sculpted in 1552 by Pietro da Salò, are set above the entryway. De Zan preserved the simple original layout of the existing building, consisting of two halls and a sacristy, and moved the great paintings (1502–07) by Vittore Carpaccio to the ground floor, placing them in a hall with wooden wainscoting where they still hang today. The nine large canvases, which recount the stories of the three patron saints of the Dalmatian Nation—St. George, St. Trifone, and St. Jerome—constitute a crucial phase in Carpaccio's artistic development. We see here a strong independence in use of color, a vibrant palette, and an interplay of light and shadow and nuanced shades, indicating a new-found freedom that not even Bellini or Giorgione had dared. Note the fanciful Eastern architecture in the scene of St. George with the dragon, taken from prints of the period by Reuwich and Breidenbach. Carpaccio's scenes acquire value as historical documents concerning dress and customs in Venice in the early Renaissance.

In the Vision of St. Augustine (opposite) the saint is shown isolated in the quiet of his study, apparently removed from the concerns of the world. The careful calligraphy and sophisticated realism of the Flemish painters combine with an architectural and airy conception of space, clearly Tuscan in origin, while the atmosphere is somehow mysterious. The objects depicted have symbolic meanings alluding to the rediscovered harmony between religious and secular studies. For example, the liturgical dress in the cabinet beneath the altar is spacially linked with the astrolabe alongside the window on the right, a symbol of scientific research. The exposed sheet music, moreover, has been identified as the notes of a hymn, and of a secular, popular song.

Scuola Grande di San Marco

Established in 1260, this headquarters of a religious brotherhood was one of the six Scuole Grandi of Venice. Following a fire in 1485, the reconstruction of the building (which now houses the Ospedale Civile, or city hospital) was entrusted to Pietro Lombardo, with the assistance of his sons and Antonio Buora. It was, however, Mauro Codussi who took over as the head of construction in 1490, and completed the building in 1495. The curvilinear crowning elements are strongly suggestive of Codussi's style,

and clearly refer to the large arches of the Basilica di San Marco. The asymmetrical exterior layout corresponds to the distribution of the interior: the highest vertical order which holds the principal portal (probably by Buora) opens onto the atrium and the upper hall (or chapel, now a private library, opposite); the right section of the facade corresponds to the residential rooms. The Scuola was deeply integrated with the politics of the Serenissima, and took part in the race for splendor and visual celebration—

strongly criticized in those Venetian milieux that supported religious reform—that sprang out of the reconstruction of the Scuole Grandi between the fifteenth and sixteenth centuries. Unlike the elite and selective approach seen in the Scuola Grande di San Giovanni Evangelista, the style selected for the Scuola di San Marco is clearly picturesque, from the local "popular" tradition.

Scuola Grande di San Rocco

Headquarters of a confraternity founded in 1478, this building was designed in its general lines by Bartolomeo Bon, who also completed the ground floor with its broad Codussi-style twin windows, between 1515 and 1524. The facade overlooking the water was the work of the Lombardo family, while Scarpagnino, between 1527 and 1549, completed the facade overlooking the square with a twofold order of Corinthian columns in the style of Sansovino. Work on the building was completed by Girolamo de' Grigi in 1560. The hall on the ground floor is punctuated by a double line of fluted Corinthian columns set on polygonal podiums of polychrome marble. The altar at the far end houses a statue of Saint Roch, the work of Gerolamo Campagna in 1587. Eight canvases by Tintoretto, completed between 1581 and 1587, adorn the walls. The Flight into Egypt (opposite), like the other artworks, shows an audacious conception of color. Light is once again the central consideration in Saint Mary of Egypt, one painting of a pair with Saint Mary Magdalene. The series dedicated to the incarnation of Christ begins with the Annunciation, and Tintoretto's visionary power is evident in the Adoration of the Shepherds. Next come the Gathering the Manna and the Baptism of Christ. The enormous upper hall, featuring wooden stalls and baroque carvings, features another twenty-three paintings by Tintoretto, done between 1575 and 1581.

Relocated at the turn of the fourteenth century to an area near the church of San Giovanni Evangelista (dedicated to St. John the Evangelist), with the sponsorship of the Badoer family, the Scuola was installed in an existing Gothic building. In 1481 Pietro Lombardo constructed the proto-Renaissance marble partition with its curvilinear pediment. It is emblazoned with an eagle, symbol of John the Evangelist, and surmounted by a cross in commemoration of the renowned relic that Filippo de' Masseris, chancellor of the kingdom of Cyprus, donated to the religious brotherhood in 1369. This building, with late-fifteenth-century modifications by Mauro Codussi and with a Lombardesque portal, forms a sort of open-air room, punctuated by rigorous Renaissance pilaster strips.

Inside, the majestic double-flight staircase was built in 1498 by Mauro Codussi, who succeeded here in making the most of the confined space available to him. Topped by a vaulted ceiling with exquisite niello decorations, the staircase is lit by a classical Codussi-style twin window, punctuated by an oculus, and inscribed in a round-head arch. The Sala Capitolare, or chapter hall (opposite), the largest room in the building, is decorated with seventeenth-century artworks by Sante Peranda, Domenico Tintoretto, and Andrea Vicentino, and sculptures by Giammaria Morlaiter; the ceiling was decorated in the eighteenth century by Giuseppe Angeli, Jacopo Guarana, Michele Marieschi, Gaspare Diziani, and Giandomenico Tiepolo. The hall was built in 1727 by Giorgio Massari, and later enriched in 1753 with an inlaid floor of polychrome marble.

The current layout and installation of the museum is the work of Carlo Scarpa, who was in charge of the project between 1945 and 1948, with further work in 1960.

There are a great many masterpieces here, ranging from the Gothic paintings of Paolo Veneziano and the Vivarini family to the Tempest by Giorgione and the large paintings of the Stories of St. Ursula by Carpaccio (pages 214–15), works by the Bellini family, Titian, and Lorenzo Lotto, and also including Giovan Battista Piazzetta, Tiepolo, and the Guardi and Longhi families.

Particularly noteworthy is the section devoted to the second half of the Venetian sixteenth century, in which, among works by Jacopo Tintoretto and the Palmas, we should mention the splendid Banquet in the House of Levi (below) executed in 1573 by Paolo Veronese for the Dominican brothers of the Santi Giovanni e Paolo. This remarkable painting, with its worldly air of an aristocratic banquet, handsome furniture, classical architecture, guests and servants, won the painter an audience with the Holy Office on a charge of suspected heresy. In order to avoid dire consequences, Veronese was forced to give the painting its current title, abandoning its original title, The Last Supper.

216

The invasion of baroque culture

Giusto Le Court, Church of Santa
Maria della Salute, main altar.

Ca' Rezzonico

This palazzo, designed by Baldassarre Longhena in 1667 on behalf of the Priuli Bon family, was completed with an additional story by Giorgio Massari between 1750 and 1758 for the Rezzonico family, who had come into ownership of the building in the meantime. The tripartite scheme of the building, traditionally linked to Sansovino, was endowed with a distinctly sculptural architectural language. The two upper floors feature great centered-arch windows emblazoned with masks and sculptures set in the extrados. The attic is perforated with a series of oculi punctuated with short fluted pilaster strips. The piano nobile is reached via the monumental staircase, and culminates in a lavish ballroom that hosted glittering fêtes right up until the 1930s. The building passed from the hands of the patrician Rezzonico family through a number of owners, among them the English poet Robert Browning, and finally Count Hirschel de' Minerbi, who sold the palazzo to the municipality of Venice in 1935. It now houses the Museo del Settecento Veneziano (Museum of Eighteenth-Century Venice) and features exquisite collections of art and furnishings.

The halls of the Museo del Settecento Veneziano were decorated in the mid-eighteenth century by such artists as Giambattista Tiepolo, Jacopo Guarana, and Giovan Battista Crosato. Trompe-l'oeil architectural views give the interiors a sense of spaciousness. The walls are arrayed with sculpture and furniture representing the celebrated, fine carving done here between 1700 and 1723 by Antonio Brustolon, prince of sculptors in wood. The master carver worked in such precious hardwoods as ebony and boxwood, creating statues of Moors contorted in exaggerated poses. The Sala del Tiepolo, named after the creator of the ceiling art, which originally hung in Palazzo Minotto Barbarigo, also features chairs carved by Brustolon. Small paintings of the Venetian school and a portrait by Alessandro Longhi hang alongside large rocaille-style mirrors. The museum was set up in the 1930s by Nino Barbantini. Chinoiserie furniture by the Calbo Crotta family, renowned paintings by Pietro Longhi including La Polenta *(right)*, a view of ordinary people of the eighteenth century, and paintings from Longhi's school, such as the sumptuous Banquet at the Casino Nani alla Giudecca *(opposite)*, all adorn the halls of the museum. Also note the Rio dei Mendicanti *(below)* by Canaletto. Among the installations are a number of reconstructions of historic buildings and rooms, including the apothecary shop known as Ai Due San Marchi, *and the rococo bedroom of Palazzo Carminati.*

Ca' Pesaro

This ambitious building is the result of
the joining of three different buildings
in a well modeled and sumptuous
array of baroque decorations. Clearly
the building was meant to extol the
magnificence of the Pesaro family,
which attained its highest point during
the doge-ship of Giovanni Pesaro,
whose rule began in 1652.
Only the ground floor, with its
diamond-shaped rustication, and the
second story, with a theatrical flair
typical of the seventeenth century, can
be said to favor the traditional
tripartite layout established by
Sansovino. These floors were
completed by Baldassarre Longhena,
who died in 1682. Succeeding him
was Antonio Gaspari, who twenty
years later erected the third story. The
building then became the property of
the Gradenigo family, and in the
nineteenth century came into the hands
of the duchess Felicita Bevilacqua La
Masa, who in turn left it to the people
of Venice upon her death in 1889.
Since 1902 it has housed the Galleria
Internazionale d'Arte Moderna, a
gallery of modern art, and since 1923,
the Museo Orientale, a museum of
Eastern art.

The Galleria d'Arte Moderna offers a remarkable documentation of the world of the great artists of the nineteenth and twentieth centuries in Italy and around the world through paintings such as Gustav Klimt's Judith, works from such schools as the Blaue Reiter and the Neue Sachlichkeit, paintings by Matisse, and by the surrealists. Ca' Pesaro also possesses a collection in which one can follow the development of "modern" art in Venice: from Francesco Hayez through Ippolito Caffi, Giacomo Favretto, and Federico Zandomeneghi and on into the novecento with the Scuola di Burano and Arturo Martini, coming to the present day with Giuseppe Santomaso and Emilio Vedova. Founded in 1897, the museum was established here in 1902. The old salon arrangement reflected the collection's formation by purchases from the various Venice Biennales and private donations; the current installation, which is more rational and up-to-date, dates back to 1983.

Palazzo Balbi

This building has been attributed to Alessandro Vittoria, a sculptor and pupil of Jacopo Sansovino. The palazzo overlooks the Grand Canal at a point where even today historic regattas start and finish. All the greatest Venetian view painters—Luca Carlevarijs, Giuseppe Baroni, Michele Marieschi, and Antonio Canaletto, as well as Antonio Visentini—have depicted this impressive palazzo over the centuries. The palazzo is considered a transitional work foreshadowing the baroque, and the structure is a compendium of sixteenth-century architectural elements. It was probably built between 1582 and 1591; in the latter year, in Nicolò Balbi's last will and testament, reference is made to the palazzo as a structurally complete building. It has a Mannerist facade that, in a welter of proto-baroque decoration, emulates the classic balustered multi-sectioned window taken from Jacopo Sansovino and the broken pediments reminiscent of Andrea Palladio. On the classic tripartite Venetian facade the structural elements fit together quite handsomely. The rustication of the ground floor is punctured by three pronounced portals surmounted by curvilinear or triangular broken pediments like the windows on the upper floors. The three-part windows on the two main floors are emphasized by twinned Ionic columns and powerful jutting balconies. Magnificent carved heraldic crests decorate the spaces between the two single side windows on the second floor, and the two obelisks on the roof are symbols of the Capitani da Mar.

The Belloni family was welcomed into the aristocracy of Venice in 1647, and purchased a fourteenth-century building on the Grand Canal; they immediately set about renovating the building, and completed the work only in 1663. On the piano nobile the facade is punctuated by a five-part window, which is flanked by two other windows topped by broken pediments, and reminiscent of the architectural style of Baldassarre Longhena; it is thought that Longhena designed this building. Set between the windows are two baroque heraldic crests with the escutcheon of the Belloni family; from the Belloni family, the palazzo passed by marriage to the Battaglia family, and in 1804 they sold it to the merchant Antonio Capovilla. Capovilla spent the enormous sum of one hundred thousand ducats to give the interior the neoclassical appearance that still distinguishes it. In the main room of the palazzo the figure painter Giambattista Canal and the ornamentalist Davide Rossi frescoed a trompe-l'oeil colonnaded atrium with a series of Homeric scenes. The symmetrical placement of the characters and the chilly colors of the fresco, mingling Tiepolesque influences and more modern Canovian inspirations, clearly show that by this point neoclassicism was triumphant in Venice. In a hall that overlooks the Canalazzo the decoration is charged with an Anglo-French flavor: the ceiling, which features false monochrome reliefs taken from Mantegna's Triumphs and stuccoes inspired by the ceramic creations of Josiah Wedgwood, is a work of art that resembles in spirit the more recent neoclassical creations of Europe.

Originally built in the fourteenth century, this building underwent a transformation into simplified baroque forms in the seventeenth century under the guidance of Antonio Gaspari. Palazzo Giustinian became the residence of the bishop of Torcello following the transfer of the episcopal see to Murano in 1707 at the behest of Marco Giustinian, and served that function until 1805. In 1840 it was transformed into a municipal office building, and then converted in 1861 to house the Museo Vetrario (glass museum) established by the abbot Zanetti. The island of Murano was renowned as early as the thirteenth century for the fine glass that was produced there; in 1291 the master glassblowers of Venice were ordered by the Doge to move their shops and furnaces to Murano, officially to prevent the fires that were caused in the city by their furnaces, but actually as a strategic move to tighten the Venetian monopoly on a unique and exceedingly profitable art. The collections of the museum concentrate on the Murano school of blown glass, whose secrets were jealously kept for centuries by master artisans who enjoyed almost aristocratic privileges. Among the remarkable items on exhibit are the famed fifteenth-century Barovier wedding goblet and a spectacular eighteenth-century centerpiece. Also noteworthy are the remarkable rococo chandeliers, especially those by Giuseppe Briati, an innovator who introduced the Bohemian style to Murano, so enraging his fellow glassblowers that, in 1739, they attacked his workshop. Through a special order issued by the Venetian Senato, Briati was allowed to set up shop in Venice, the first glassblower to do so in five centuries.

Palazzo Giustinian Lolin

Built between the fourteenth and fifteenth centuries in the Gothic style, this palazzo was renovated between 1623 and 1625 at the behest of Giovanni Lolin, who left a considerable sum of money to his son-in-law Giovanni Giustinian to rebuild the palazzo in compliance with the artistic demands of the period. The renovation, one of the earliest assignments in Venice for the young Baldassarre Longhena, produced a simple, linear facade entirely faced in Istrian stone, yet exceedingly refined in its elegant structural details, its beautifully balanced balconies, the pilaster strips, and the graphic interplay of the cornices. The ground floor, devoid of the classic mezzanine, appears rather low, and seems insufficient to sustain the facade. The unusual height of the windows was a response to the structural demands posed by the existing Gothic apertures, and the facade shows the influence of Vincenzo Scamozzi, especially in the centered windows. Once the home of the duchess of Parma, the palazzo was later purchased by Ugo and Olga Levi, who assembled a remarkable collection of musical scores, now preserved here in the foundation that bears their names.

This building, which dates to about 1560, is pictured in the background of a renowned painting by Paolo Veronese (1571) of the Virgin Mary with the Coccina family, who had the building constructed. The painting is now in Dresden. Originally from Bergamo, the Coccina were a family of exceedingly wealthy merchants, and were great clients of Paolo Veronese—they also commissioned three other canvases of great renown. They hired Giangiacomo de' Grigi from Bergamo, the son of Guglielmo de' Grigi, to design their palazzo. The facade is clearly designed by someone mindful of the precepts of Sebastiano Serlio, and is punctuated at the center by two Serlian windows, one atop the other, and marked by powerful courses at each story. It also displays classical inspirations from the work of Michele Sanmicheli, and from the architecture of the late Venetian cinquecento.

In 1864 the palazzo became the property of the counts of Papadopoli-Aldobrandini who, ten years later, had the interior redecorated in a luxurious eclectic style by the antiquarian Michelangelo Guggenheim. Since 1922, the palazzo has been owned by the counts of Arrivabene.

Ca' Zenobio

The long baroque facade of the palazzo, built along the Rio dei Carmini between 1690 and 1700 by the architect Antonio Gaspari, conceals a C-shaped floor plan. A curvilinear pediment clearly inspired by the work of Francesco Borromini—Gaspari was perhaps the only Venetian architect of this period to sense the allure of the baroque style being used in Rome by Bernini and Borromini—enlivens the flat series of windows in the attic, while a more classical Serlian window interrupts the line of the piano nobile.

At the far end of the garden, once crisscrossed by boxwood shrubbery, Tomaso Temanza built a pavilion at the end of the eighteenth century in precocious neoclassical style, and meant for use as an archive and library.

Notable figures of the local school of painters lent their talents in the decoration of the official reception areas. Among them were Gregorio Lazzarini, a young apprentice named Giambattista Tiepolo, and Luca Carlevarijs, the first great Venetian view painter, who did the three landscapes in the main hall, and was so involved with this project that he was commonly known as Luca di Ca' Zenobio. The ballroom on the piano nobile was sumptuously decorated with glittering white-and-gold stuccoes—probably the work of the Ticino artist Abbondio Stazio— which adorn doors and windows in floral garlands, bas-reliefs, complex moldings, and full-fledged sculptures of putti, with a theatrical, late-baroque impact. In counterpoint to these is the trompe-l'oeil perspective of the "bottomless" ceiling, the work of the exuberant Lodovico Dorigny, who frescoed the ceiling with dwarfs, powerful foreshortened nudes, urns, Oriental carpets, and allegories, in a concerted exaltation of the Zenobio heraldic crest.

The palazzo is now the headquarters of the college of the Armenian Mechitarist fathers.

Palazzo Michiel dalle Colonne

In the place of an original Veneto-Byzantine building, the architect Antonio Gaspari, proponent in Venice of the new Roman baroque style at the end of the seventeenth century, established a new architectural composition. Alongside the broad Serlian windows are apertures crowned by broken semicircular pediments containing busts in relief. Only the portico testifies to the original structure of the palazzo. Originally owned by the Grimani family, the building passed into the hands of the Zeno family, and in 1707, to the Duke of Mantua, and then to the Michiel family.

Palazzo Moro-Lin

This palazzo was built in 1670 by a Tuscan painter, Sebastiano Mazzoni, for a client who was also a painter—the renowned Pietro Liberi. Also known as "the palazzo with thirteen windows," the building represents the transformation of two existing Gothic buildings.

The entire façade is rusticated and is punctuated by a continual series of windows, with pilaster strips and capitals in three different orders. The top story was added in 1703, disturbing the harmonious proportions of the building. The building later became the property of the Lin family, originally from Bergamo, who bought their way into the Venetian aristocracy in 1686; marriage brought the palazzo into the estate of the Moro family in 1788. It was frescoed in several different phases by such artists as Antonio Bellucci, Antonio Molinari, Gregorio Lazzarini, and Luca Carlevarijs in the eighteenth century and by Carlo Bevilacqua and Pietro Moro in the nineteenth century. Sadly, not a trace of their work survives today.

In the first half of the nineteenth century, the artists Francesco Hayez and Ludovico Lipparini had their studios in this palazzo.

239

Until fairly recent times, the method of entry into Venice was by water. When cargo vessels entered the city through the Bacino Marciano, they would stop to clear their cargoes through customs at the appropriate office, which was located on the easternmost strip of land of the Sestiere di Dorsoduro.
In 1677, Giuseppe Benoni, winner of a competition for the reconstruction of the existing fourteenth-century structure, erected a square tower in Istrian stone, bound on three sides by a portico with stout rusticated columns. High atop this tower perches a group of bronzes by the Ticinese sculptor Bernardo Falcone. The group comprises two Atlases supporting the well known golden sphere, upon which is balanced an allegorical figure of Fortune.

Church of the Scalzi

The job of rebuilding in a larger baroque version the unassuming church of the Carmelitani Scalzi (Barefoot Carmelites), dedicated to Saint Mary of Nazareth, was entrusted to Baldassarre Longhena in 1660. But it was Giuseppe Sardi, in 1672, who completed the exterior facade, which fairly swarms with decorations, while the interior—the work of the lay Carmelite Fra Giuseppe Pozzo, brother of the better-known Andrea Pozzo—was faced in polychrome marble in a baroque apotheosis culminating in the enormous machinery of the main altar. In 1743 Giambattista Tiepolo painted the vault with the Transportation of the Holy House of Loreto, a fresco that was destroyed in 1915 in an Austrian bombardment; only a sketch of it survives, in the Gallerie dell'Accademia. The major decorative projects were undertaken and financed by the Friulian family of the Manin, a recent addition to the Venetian nobility, who pursued ambitious ends partly through religious sponsorship.

The last doge of the Venetian Republic, Lodovico Manin, who was deposed in 1797, is buried here.

Built on an existing medieval structure in 1668 by Alessandro Tremignon, this church dominates the straightaway of one of the major modern projects of urban renovation in Venice: the nineteenth-century Via XXII Marzo. The emphatic baroque facade—marked by an exuberant, composite ornamentation peopled with sculptures by the Flemish artist Heinrich Meyring that overflow over the tripartite post-Palladian geometry—was conceived as an affirmation of patrician pride. The recently ennobled Fini brothers, who lived in a nearby palazzo on the Grand Canal, spent the considerable sum of thirty thousand ducats to build the church. Busts of the brothers, one set atop the central obelisk, emerge from the theatrical composition of statues and cornices, while the family crest stands out against the rough marble surface of the pediment, where the extreme baroque decorations and the horror vacui dwindle into the powerful form of the cornice.

Church of the Jesuits
(Santa Maria Assunta)

After the Jesuits were readmitted to Venice in 1657, they took up residence in the suppressed convent complex of the Crociferi, and rebuilt the medieval church. Between 1715 and 1728 Domenico Rossi, with the assistance of Giovanni Battista Fattoretto, built this house of worship, whose facade is a Jesuit prototype. The interior, laid out lengthwise with deep side chapels, is adorned with stuccoes by Abbondio Stazio working in collaboration with Tencalla. The trompe-l'oeil brocade on the walls behind the theatrical pulpit bears the heraldic colors of the Manin family, who sponsored the construction and were closely tied to the Jesuits. Dominating the presbytery is the sumptuous, baroque main altar designed by Fra' Giuseppe Pozzo and composed of ten tortile columns made of verde antico marble supporting a perforated dome: a resolutely Roman piece of architecture directly inspired by the designs of Andrea Pozzo, a member of the Company of Jesus, and an architectural interpreter of its precepts. Among the paintings by Tintoretto, Jacopo Palma the Younger, and Pietro Liberi, the church possesses the Martyrdom of Saint Lawrence by Titian (opposite), a visionary, expressionistic composition dating from 1559 in which the dramatic nocturnal scene shows a vibrant colorism that even Tintoretto would not have dared to attempt. One relic of the older church of the Crociferi is the colossal sixteenth-century monument built by Jacopo Sansovino to glorify the noble da Lezze family. To the left of the main altar, a monument completed in 1595 by Gerolamo Campagna commemorates the Doge Pasquale Cicogna.

Ospedaletto

Founded in 1527 as a charitable institution for penniless invalids and the elderly, this hospice has a history closely bound to musical composition, especially in the eighteenth century. Young guests here were instructed in the musical arts under the tutelage of illustrious masters, among them Nicolò Porpora, Tommaso Traetta, Pasquale Anfossi, and above all Domenico Cimarosa, who was the glory of the remarkable artistic history of the eighteenth century and the history of this hospital. The elliptically shaped music hall built by Matteo Lucchesi was set aside for the concerts of the young girls, who are depicted there in trompe-l'oeil choirs. The hall was frescoed in 1776 by Jacopo Guarana with allegories that refer to its function, set among architectural illusions by Agostino Mengozzi Colonna. Adjacent to the music hall is the oval staircase built to plans by Giuseppe Sardi and completed by Baldassarre Longhena. The baroque façade of the adjoining church, begun by Sardi in 1667, was completed in 1674 by Longhena. The façade features a number of grotesque pillars which transform into unsettling herm-like figures, while contorted telamons support the trabeation. The entire façade was designed as a cenotaph for the client Bartolomeo Carnioni. Inside the rectangular hall is a notable collection of seventeenth- and eighteenth-century paintings and sculptures, including work by Giambattista Pittoni, Carlo Maria Loth, Andrea Celesti, and Giambattista Tiepolo.

This church is also known as Santa Maria Zobenigo, after the name of the Jubanico family, which founded it in the tenth century. The present baroque facade is the work of Giuseppe Sardi, who completed it between 1678 and 1683. The double order of twinned Ionic and Corinthian half-columns is topped by a small pediment, and statues by Giusto Le Court crowd the silhouette of the building. The Barbaro family commissioned this work, and the church is a sort of celebratory monument to the gens, or clan—a fairly rare occurrence in baroque Venice, when the mentality of the aristocracy was still oriented toward the traditional mediocritas. In the center of the middle order is the glorious effigy of the Capitano da Mar Antonio Barbaro, set on a pedestal, gripping his staff of command—a clear indication of the encomiastic significance of the entire decorative array. Also oriented toward a glorification of the deeds and prestigious political offices of Antonio Barbaro are the six bas-relief plans of cities (Zara, Candia, Padua, Rome, Corfu, and Split) which adorn the lower stylobate. The rectangular interior, with a single nave enriched by a flat ceiling adorned with baroque paintings by Antonio Zanchi, is bedecked with numerous paintings, among them artworks by Francesco Salviati, Jacopo and Domenico Tintoretto, Carlo Maria Loth, Giovan Battista Piazzetta, Andrea Schiavone, Jacopo Palma the Younger, and Peter Paul Rubens. Also in keeping with the baroque splendor of the structure are the remarkable marble decorations of an altarpiece, carried over to the marble intarsia floors.

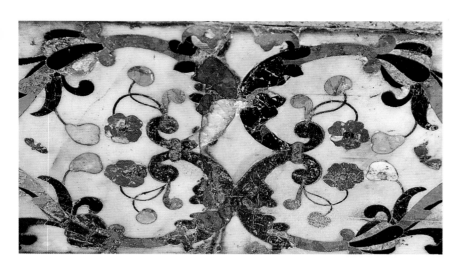

This cathedral, erected by Baldassarre Longhena beginning in 1631, is the most renowned and theatrical manifestation of the baroque in Venice. The basilica was built in compliance with a vow led by the Doge Contarini and taken by the entire populace of Venice, to the Virgin Mary in thanksgiving for the end of the terrible plague that had killed thousands the year before, a vow that even today is profoundly felt and deeply respected with a traditional pilgrimage on 21 November. The church stands triumphantly at the very end of the Grand Canal, its impressive cupola supported by powerful and elegant spiraling volutes surmounted by sculptures.

The interior is built to a central plan with a continuous circular peribolos—a clear reference to early-Christian and Byzantine models. As in the Redentore, the other great votive church of the city, the presbytery is defined by two central, semicircular apses. Among the numerous artworks by Titian, Luca Giordano, Sassoferrato, and Tintoretto, the elaborate, baroque main altar by Giusto Le Court houses a twelfth-century Byzantine icon, the greatly venerated Virgin of Mesopanditissa brought from Candia by the Doge Morosini in 1672. The floor, made of polychrome marble tiles, is punctuated with inlaid roses (symbols of the Virgin Mary) and Stars of David, which allude to Mary's descent from the Hebrew king. The design extends in concentric waves from the central disk, which bears the legend in Latin unde origo inde salus, sealing the association of Venice and the Virgin Mary, whose feast day (the Annunciation, 25 March) falls on the day on which the city is said to have been founded in 421.

Baldassarre Longhena, the greatest architect of the Venetian baroque, worked on this building in two separate phases—the first between 1627 and 1663, the second between 1668 and 1670—establishing a facade with two orders of half-columns set on plinths. The side elevation features a broad rusticated socle, with two portals topped by pediments. The rectangular interior is rich in baroque and rococo decorations. The exquisite aesthetic of this Scuola is represented by the splendid decoration of the salone, or great hall. The marble floor, the altar, and above all, the paintings form a unique, late-baroque artistic complex. The ceiling is renowned first and foremost as the work of Giambattista Tiepolo, but one should not overlook the artwork by Tiepolo's master Gregorio Lazzarini, nor the paintings by Antonio Zanchi. Tiepolo's ceiling (following pages), completed between 1739 and 1749, is divided into nine sections, and emphasizes pale hues of white, turquoise, pink, and green. Its colorism reaches its high point in the lovely central canvas in which the Virgin Mary hands a scapular to the blessed Simone Stock. All around, angels in flight and evanescent clouds imbue the scene with an exquisite harmony of light and shade. The stucco decorations of the graceful vaults over the staircase are by the Ticinese artist Abbondio Stazio, and the frescoed tondos from the early eighteenth century are by Sante Piatti.

Scuola Levantina

This building, clearly inspired by the style of Baldassarre Longhena, was built between 1683 and 1700 for a community of Levantine Jews—a term used to indicate Jews from the Iberian peninsula and from various areas of the Ottoman empire—who were a particularly influential tribe, though few in number, within the Venetian Ghetto. The interior of the hall, with its heavy baroque furnishings, is without a doubt the most sumptuous setting in the Ghetto. The hall culminates overhead in the matronaeum, or women's gallery, which is screened off by wooden gratings. The many bronze lamps that hang from the ceiling were a gift from the Jewish community of Amsterdam for the new temple. The carved ceiling and the bimah—a sort of pulpit from which prayers and benedictions were given— are said to have been the work of the renowned cabinetmaker Antonio Brustolon, a virtuoso of baroque wood carving. The bimah, teeming with ornament, seems to have been meant to join the liturgical requirements of the Jewish religion with the splendor of baroque style; note the two tortile columns, reminiscent of the work of Gianlorenzo Bernini.

The eighteenth century:
the final triumph

Ca' Zenobio.
Decoration of the salone.

Palazzo Grassi

A patrician residence of the late Republic, this palazzo was begun on behalf of the Grassi family by Giorgio Massari in 1748, and after his death was not completed until 1772. The spectacular building, which emulates the layout of Ca' Corner, winds around a colonnaded courtyard with a second-floor loggia. The three-flight staircase features decorations by Michelangelo Morleiter, in which ladies and gentlemen in masks lean through illusionistic windows. The ceiling contains the tributary fresco, the Apotheosis of the Grassi family, attributed to Fabio Canal. After a radical restoration by Gae Aulenti in 1984 on behalf of a private company, the building now houses major art exhibitions.

Palazzo Labia

Among the most extreme examples of baroque layout and the stylistic approach established by Baldassarre Longhena, this palazzo was built at the turn of the eighteenth century by Alessandro Tremignon. Tremignon was replaced by Andrea Cominelli, who completed the work in 1720. The palazzo stands at the confluence of the Rio di Cannaregio with the Grand Canal. A classical double order of windows punctuates the two main stories, laid out neatly between the massive rustication on the ground floor and the attic riddled with oculi set off by eagles, the heraldic emblem of the Labia family. The Labia were exceedingly wealthy merchants of Catalonian origin, who were admitted to the Venetian aristocracy in 1647. They became major protagonists in the social life of the eighteenth century, and their banquets and parties were unrivaled. The high banquets were said to culminate in the tossing of gold and silver tablesettings into the canal below. Particularly remarkable is the frescoed decoration of the salone, or great hall; these frescoes were done by Giambattista Tiepolo between about 1746 and 1749 in collaboration with the trompe-l'oeil artist Girolamo Mengozzi. The powerful colorism, the grandeur and brilliance of the visual language, the evident nostalgia for fifteenth-century Venetian painting, all come to a crescendo in the Banquet of Anthony and Cleopatra, truly the focal point of the entire visual narrative. In 1951 the last owner of the palazzo, Carlos Besteigui, hosted a masked ball that for one short night revived the spectacular decadence of the eighteenth-century Serenissima.

This church was once part of the Ospedale dei Mendicanti founded at the end of the sixteenth century, one of the nine major charitable institutions in the city of Venice at the time. It is now the property of the city hospital. Begun to a design by Vincenzo Scamozzi in 1633, the church was given a neo-Palladian façade by Giuseppe Sardi in 1664—the beginning of a revival of this architectural style. The large vestibule that extends before the hall was designed to muffle sounds from outside during concerts of the putte, young female musicians who were a major attraction here, as in other charitable institutions in the city.

On the rear façade stands a monument designed by Giuseppe Sardi to Alvise Mocenigo, a philanthropist and the heroic defender of Candia. It was executed in 1658 with sculptures by Giusto Le Court and reliefs by John Bushnell, and its glittering baroque opulence represents that of the interior of the building as well. Among the paintings by Paolo Veronese and Jacopo Tintoretto is the only painting by Guercino in all of Venice: Saint Helena Adoring the True Cross.

Palazzo Sagredo

This building has a fourteenth-century Gothic layout, and echoes the standard Byzantine format in the six-part window on the second floor. Once the property of the Morosini family, it was taken over in the early eighteenth century by Gherardo Sagredo, who summoned Abbondio Stazio and the Tencalla in 1718 to do the stuccoes of the high mezzanine, while a spectacular staircase by Andrea Tirali rose in the atrium, presumably complete by 1734 when Pietro Longhi completed his Fall of the Giants fresco on the ceiling. Tomaso Temanza's ambitious plans, dated 1738, to rebuild the palazzo in a classical style remained a dead letter. Following the dispersal of the rich collection of paintings, in 1906 Ca' Sagredo underwent the further loss of an alcove adorned with virtuoso stuccoes, one of the most remarkable rooms of the Venetian late baroque, probably done by Stazio, and now in the Metropolitan Museum of Art in New York. The paintings in the main hall on the second floor, done in 1773, are the work of Andrea Urbani, a well-known painter and stage designer.

Church of the Tolentini
(San Nicolò da Tolentino)

The Padri Teatini, or Theatine
Fathers, who fled Rome after the Sack
of 1527, established themselves in the
Oratorio di San Nicolò da Tolentino
in 1528. As the order grew in
importance, the decision was made to
build a church and a monastery.
Andrea Palladio produced a design
that was not built, but which greatly
influenced the final eighteenth-century
building, which was entrusted to
Vincenzo Scamozzi in 1591. The
layout of the church is clearly inspired
by Palladio's work: a Latin-cross
nave with three chapels along each
side and an elongated presbytery
opening from it. Behind the somewhat
theatrical main altar by Baldassarre
Longhena, with sculptures by Giusto
Le Court, is the choir loft of the monks.
There is a notable array of artworks:
paintings by Bonifacio Pitati,
Leandro Bassano, Jacopo Palma the
Younger, Bernardo Strozzi, and Luca
Giordano, and a seventeenth-century
monument to the Patriarch Francesco
Morosini, by the sculptor Filippo
Parodi. The tambour over the cross-
vault is enclosed by a ceiling with
frescoes by Gaetano Zompini and
Mengozzi Colonna. Between 1706
and 1714 Andrea Tirali added a
pronaos with Corinthian columns,
topped by a pediment to the brickwork
facade.

Rebuilt in 1678 by Giovanni Grassi,
with a rectangular nave and three
chapels on either side, this church is
covered by a vaulted ceiling and is lit
by a double order of windows. The
facade was completed in 1709 with a
bequest from the Mocenigo family. It
was built by Domenico Rossi, who, in
a single year, put up an elevation with
giant Corinthian columns set on tall
plinths, supporting the pediment and
providing a transition between the
decorative baroque style and the neo-
Palladianism of the eighteenth century.
Sebastiano Ricci frescoed the ceiling of
the presbytery, and thanks to the
bequest of the aristocrat Andrea
Stazio, twelve canvases of the Apostles
were commissioned from twelve artists,
thus creating a full-fledged anthology
of Venetian painting of the eighteenth
century. This features the nuanced and
luminous colorism of Sebastiano Ricci
in the Liberation of Saint Peter,
the violent chiaroscuro of Saint
James by Giovan Battista Piazzetta,
and the Martyrdom of Saint
Bartholomew, a vivid drama set in
dark shadows by the young Tiepolo.

Church of the Gesuati (Santa Maria del Rosario)

Built by Giorgio Massari between 1726 and 1736 on behalf of the Dominican Order—the order that took over following the suppression of the Gesuati—this church overlooks the Zattere with a tripartite elevation and tall Corinthian columns, clear references to the work of Palladio, as is the pediment above them. The interior features a single nave punctuated by Corinthian half-columns, rich, geometric marble-inlay flooring and a main altar with a lapis lazuli tabernacle.

Filled with works of art by Venice's greatest masters, especially of the eighteenth century, the church features a ceiling decorated by the young Giambattista Tiepolo between 1737 and 1739, with frescoes and grisailles concerning subjects particular to the Dominican Order. The central panel is The Apparition of the Virgin Mary Before Saint Dominick (page 271), a fresco in a symphony of pale greens, pinks, and pearly grays, standing out between the translucent skies and the powerful presence of the figures in the foreground. Other frescoes by Tiepolo adorn the presbytery, while paintings by Tintoretto, Giovan Battista Piazzetta, and Sebastiano Ricci, including his Pius V between Saint Thomas and Saint Peter (opposite), complete the array of paintings. There is yet another masterpiece by Tiepolo, an altarpiece depicting The Virgin Mary and Saint Catherine of Siena, Saint Rosa of Lima, and Saint Agnes of Montepulciano (right), which was commissioned in 1740 and is portrayed in a solemn and classical manner. This work of Tiepolo's serves as a sharp counterpoint to the impetuous power that reverberates through the frescoes, even though he finished them only the previous year.

Following the demolition of the existing thirteenth-century building, this refined and rigorous structure in the neoclassical style was rebuilt ex novo around 1760 by Tomaso Temanza, who was more of a historian and theoretician of the new rationalist architectural styles than he was a practicing architect. Temanza, who had been affected by the writing of Father Carlo Lodoli, was the most authentic precursor of neoclassicism in the Venice area, and the Church of the Maddalena was certainly the masterpiece of that art school. Situated on the Campo della Maddalena, set slightly back from the crowded Strada Nuova, the church of Santa Maria Maddalena stands out for its compact, geometric shape, established upon a circular plan and defined by the smooth white stone on the face of the church. Clearly Temanza took inspiration from the Pantheon, which a few decades earlier served as inspiration to Giovanni Scalfarotto for his church of San Simeon Piccolo. Still, the classical Roman verbum is particularly well represented here, given the assembly of a tambour and a slightly lowered dome, and the pronaos supported by pairs of Ionic columns, which seem to shrink in volume, flattening themselves against the facade. The interior has a hexagonal layout and small oratory dimensions; Temanza was buried here in 1789. There are also adjoining, outlying chapels, and a presbytery of a dynamic ovoid shape.

Church of the Pietà
(Church of the Visitazione)

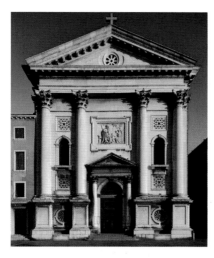

The Ospedale della Pietà, founded in
1346 to take in and educate poor
orphan girls, became in the eighteenth
century a remarkable and fertile school
of music. Antonio Vivaldi, the Red
Priest famed for the color of his hair—
whose compositions are widely
identified with the very idea of the
Serenissima in its final glory—was
the master of the chorus and the violin
here from 1703 on; he wrote most of
his lifework for this institution. The
Palladian facade of the church was
designed by Giorgio Massari between
1744 and 1760, but was only completed, through a bequest, in 1906.
The elliptical interior culminates in the
presbytery. Along the walls, which are
punctuated by twinned pilaster strips,
lie the altars beneath rigorous windows
reminiscent of Palladio. The clearly
musical vocation of this church is dem-
onstrated by the three hanging choir
lofts with massive wrought-iron grates,
where the famous putte ospealere
(young girls of the hospital) would
sing, to the delight of such foreign
visitors as Charles de Brosses and the
Counts of the North (Czarevitch Paul
and Czarevna Feodorovna), who were
invited by the Signoria in 1782 to
enjoy a concert featuring the virtuoso
female singers of nine city hospitals.
The event was recorded by the careful
paintbrush of Gabriel Bella. The angels
that surround the apotheosis of the
Virgin Mary in the luminous fresco
Giambattista Tiepolo painted on the
ceiling of the hall (left) are also musicians. Tiepolo painted a series of
works for this church between 1754
and 1755, including a sacred allegory
that was destroyed during the completion of the facade at the turn of the
twentieth century.

Church of the Fava
(Santa Maria della
Consolazione)

The modern-day building was begun
in the early eighteenth century by
Antonio Gaspari, and replaced a
fifteenth-century oratory. Gaspari's
innovative design, clearly influenced
by the development of the Roman
baroque style, could hardly have been
accepted readily in a setting like that
of the Venetian lagoon, crystallized as
it was into the dogmatic observance of
the Palladian style. What resulted
was an elegant hall with a single aisle,
an ovoid plan with rounded angles,
and three large chapels along the sides.
The facade is incomplete. In 1750
Giorgio Massari built the presbytery
and the main altar. Aside from the
statues of saints and evangelists that
adorn eight niches among the pillars,
there are paintings by Giambettino
Cignaroli and Jacopo Amigoni, and
The Virgin Mary with Cherub
and Saint Philip Neri in Prayer,
a work from the later career of Giovan
Battista Piazzetta, who was later
buried here in the family tomb of his
friend Giambattista Albrizzi. Without
a doubt, however, the true masterpiece
of the church is the large painting
depicting The Education of the
Virgin Mary (right), the work of the
young Giambattista Tiepolo (1732).
The influence of Piazzetta has here
almost disappeared, and instead we
clearly see the powerful thrust of
Tiepolo's expressive realism, and his
substantial and radiant light. Saint
Ann, Saint Joachim, and the Virgin
Mary as a girl are enveloped in a haze
that fades from the nuance of color
typical of Piazzetta to the distinctive,
tender shades of Tiepolo. Hovering
above the figures is a baroque group of
angels by Pietro Liberi.

Sadly, the photographs on these pages correspond to nothing more than memories—the theater was destroyed for the third time in its history by a terrible fire on 29 January 1996. In the past, the theater held the name of the mythical firebird—La Fenice is Italian for Phoenix—which rises from its ashes; now one can only hope that the name and symbol help to ensure a speedy and intelligent reconstruction. The theater burned for the first time in 1773; twenty-nine plans were presented for the reconstruction of this most important theater in the city. The chosen project was by the young architect Gian Antonio Selva; it was neoclassical in style, and was distinguished by a pronaos with columns.

The facade, built between 1790 and 1792, has survived the theater's many disasters. On the interior further modifications were made in the wake of another fire, which broke out in 1836; in 1837 the Meduna brothers reworked (from the original plans by Selva) the Empire style of the foyer. And again Giambattista Meduna decorated the great hall in 1854, based on a fanciful revisitation of the eighteenth-century style: the decorations teemed with gilded moldings, and culminated in the Royal Box (1866). A late neoclassical style also distinguished the medallions with putti on the boxes and the group of figures that hovered in the heavens of the ceiling, designed in 1854 by Leonardo Gavagnin.

Neoclassical and romantic Venice

Palazzo Ziani.
Frescoes in the salone.

Coffee House

This pavilion designed by Lorenzo Santi in the context of the overall renovation of the area marciana ordered by the Napoleonic court, was built between 1815 and 1817, and constitutes an anomaly in the structural style of Venice. The structure was erected in an area that needed a new identity following the demolition of the Graneri di Terra Nova, or grain siloes. Santi, born in Siena but Roman by education, reached Venice in the wake of Giuseppe Soli, and developed a design in which (in clear contrast with the prevailing local neoclassical style) the ornamental aspects prevailed over the architecture itself. Echoes of Roman and other European styles, as well as hints of the work of Giuseppe Borsato, are mixed in this majestic architecture on a Lilliputian scale. The baseless Doric columns are emptied of power, and the overall scale is intentionally small, justified by the recreational nature of the building and its distance from the majestic giants of the nearby Piazza San Marco.

Palazzo Ziani

Pietro Moro was one of the prolific artists to emerge from the milieu of Giuseppe Borsato, leader of the Venetian neoclassical school. The figure painter Moro was active in a number of Venetian buildings, alone or in collaboration with Borsato himself, or with Carlo Bevilacqua and Davide Rossi. After his debut at Palazzo Manin in 1800 and his work on Palazzo Reale in 1807, Moro had a number of aristocratic commissions. Notable among them is Ca' Ziani at San Zulian. The salone and the adjoining rooms on the third floor are decorated with paintings of mythological subjects, trompe l'oeils, and false statues. Austere episodes of Roman history, scenes of bacchanalia, grotesques, and monochrome cameos adorn walls and ceilings, drawing on a well-known repertory used repeatedly by this artist.

Palazzo Giovanelli

This palazzo is a remarkable mixture of the flamboyant Gothic of the fifteenth century and the neo-Gothic revival. The structure was erected for the Donà family in the fifteenth century, and was restored and partly rebuilt for Count Andrea Giovanelli by Giambattista Meduna between 1847 and 1848. The elevation overlooking the water features dominant four-lobed fretwork, a reference to the pointed-arch arrangement of the Ca' d'Oro, which Meduna was restoring at the same time that he oversaw work on Palazzo Giovanelli. There is a strong medievalist style throughout the interior. Beginning with the entryway and the large octagonal stairway, lit by an elegante rose-window skylight, Meduna clearly reveals his intentions: to create a decorative universe nourished both by the local and the flamboyant Gothic.

Church of San Maurizio

Rebuilt in 1590 to replace an older church, the church was again rebuilt in 1806 by Giannantonio Selva, and completed in 1828 by Antonio Diedo. Selva took over the design from the patrician Pietro Zaguri, who apparently came up with the idea of reproducing in the new church a semblance of the demolished church of San Geminiano (by Sansovino) in Piazza San Marco.

The Greek-cross plan is reminiscent of the approach adopted by Mauro Codussi, in a layout with four vaulted wings with a central cupola. The serene façade is updated to accord with the new visual languages of nineteenth-century Europe, and is embellished with stone ashlars. Reliefs in two rectangular panels lie on the second course above the windows, and the pediment is similarly carved. Adjoining the square space of the interior sits the small semicircular apse containing grisailles by Giuseppe Borsato, and above the altar rises a refined neoclassical tabernacle by Giannantonio Selva.

This church dates back to the ninth century, and was entirely rebuilt in the neoclassical style by Lorenzo Santi in 1837. In 1843 the structure was again modified, by Giambattista Meduna, to mitigate what the clients insisted was an excessively secular approach to ecclesiastical architecture. The neoclassical interior has a single aisle joining the side alters with the main altar. Among the artwork here are a fourteenth-century polyptych, the Baptism of Christ by Jacopo Tintoretto, and Girolamo da Santacroce's picture of St. Thomas à Becket.

Cemetery of San Michele in Isola

In 1837 two islands were joined into one by filling in a canal that had once divided them. These islands were those of San Michele—where a Renaissance church stood with the adjoining Camaldolese cenoby—and San Cristoforo della Pace, which as early as 1807 had been set aside by the government of Napoleon's viceroy as the site of the city cemetery, which the new sanitary regulations stipulated must be outside of the residential section of the city. After the rejection of a number of proposed designs for the cemetery, and two competitions that produced no acceptable ideas, the architect Annibale Forcellini finally built a functional solution between 1872 and 1881. Far from the original monumental proposals, Forcellini's design was based on a horizontal development of the site in a moderate neo-Gothic style, with the occasional salient structure offering a counterpoint to the circle of walls that surround the cemetery. Clearly inspired by the painting of Arnold Böcklin, this "island of the dead" in a neo-pointed-arch vernacular was set aside as the final resting place of a number of famous individuals, who were brought here in a melancholy, veiled, funeral gondola, with an angel holding a spent torch. Among the international aristocrats and intellectuals who now rest here are Sergei Diaghilev of the Ballets Russes, Igor Stravinsky, who premiered his The Rake's Progress in Venice, and Ezra Pound, the American poet who died in 1972, and whose Cantos made him one of the most remarkable bards of the Serenissima.

Palazzo Cavalli Franchetti

This late Gothic building from the fifteenth century overlooks the Grand Canal and the Ponte dell'Accademia. In much the same way as the Palazzo Giovanelli, but with a much richer monumental dimension, Palazzo Cavalli Franchetti was set up as a confrontation between the original pointed-arch conception and the nineteenth-century revival. After an initial period under Giambattista Meduna, between 1878 and 1882 the palazzo was the subject of a restoration of the facade, and of a neo-medievalist reinvention in other areas under the supervision of Camillo Boito, assisted by Carlo Matscheg and Girolamo Manetti for the structural aspects. The great staircase, set in a cubic architectural wing, opens out toward the exterior, as if "broken through" by the broad windows on its three unencumbered sides. The iron fixtures used in the building already employ a proto-industrial vernacular.

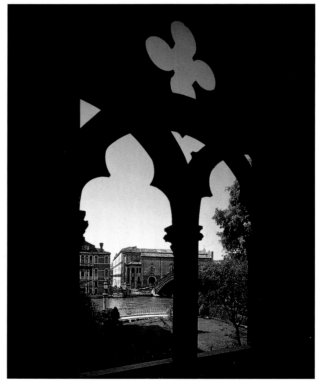

Conservation, transformation, and modernity

Carlo Scarpa, Fondazione Scientifica
Querini Stampalia, entrance.

The progress of modern architecture in Venice, a city that rejected the plans of two such modern masters as Frank Lloyd Wright and Le Corbusier, has really only resulted in a few triumphant instances, among them several of the pavilions of the Venice Biennale. Established in 1895, magnificently isolated from the city of Venice, cordoned off by water and concealed in a park that wards off the usual Venetian contextual references, between 1930 and 1965 the Biennale became a privileged and secluded site of an epiphany of the modern. The entry avenue is closed off by the Italian pavilion, which awaits reconstruction by Francesco Cellini. Also deserving of mention are the Dutch pavilion, designed and built by Gerrit Rietveld in 1954, the Finnish pavilion (right) by Alvar Aalto in 1956, and the superb Austrian pavilion (opposite) built by Josef Hoffmann in 1934. Between 1948 and 1954 Carlo Scarpa designed and built the ticket office, part of the garden of the Italian pavilion, and the Venezuelan pavilion.

Designed by Giovanni Sardi it 1908,
this hotel immediately became—along
with the nearby Hotel des Bains—one
of the most popular lodgings of elegant
cosmopolitan tourists of the turn of the
twentieth century. The long facade
enlivened by cupolas, tapering spires,
terraces, and small towers, combines
elements of the Veneto-Byzantine
tradition with Oriental references, in
particular a clear reference to the
Grand Hotel of Cairo, which was
built around the same time. Although
the interior has been roughly restored
in several areas in the recent past, it
still features original rooms such as the
large, well-lit dining room, where pale
stuccoes, lavish chandeliers, appliqués
in Murano glass, and neo-Louis XVI
furniture all combine to fulfill the
demands for luxury of the refined
clientele that made the Venetian Lido
famous during the art-nouveau era.
Along the famous beach wind two
lines of cabanas designed by Ignazio
Gardella in an Oriental style, after
the great flood of 1966 destroyed the
original cabanas.

Casa Torres

Overlooking the Rio del Gaffaro, this small building is a prime example of architectural neo-medievalism. Giuseppe Torres plundered the visual historic treasury of the city: elements of Romanesque and Veneto-Byzantine structural style, such as the series window of the facade, are juxtaposed against funnel chimneys reminiscent of the paintings of Carpaccio. Avoiding the showmanship of grander homes, this building is steeped in a well-thought-out intimism.

The Lido, the destination in the late nineteenth and early twentieth centuries of the most exclusive international tourists, was to become the setting for the second phase of Venetian romantic architecture. The fanciful adaptation of the Moorish style and the flamboyant Gothic, freed of the limiting context of their historical setting, here engenders an unusual aesthetic from which emerge the art-nouveau inventions of Torres and Guido Costante Sullam. The latter is the architect of Villa Monplaisir, built at the behest of Nicolò Spada, founder of the Compagnia Italiana Grandi Alberghi. Asymmetrical in layout, this updated art-nouveau architecture is interwoven with inspirations and styles taken from the work of Victor Horta in the same period, and from the sophisticated styling of Josef Hoffmann. The decoration is of great quality, and comprises such diverse materials as glazed polychrome ceramic, brass fittings, and wrought iron—all the work of Venetian craftsmen.

Casa del Farmacista

This pharmacy with simple, refined lines was built on the Lido in 1926–27 by Brenno Del Giudice, with a stylistic approach that even today denotes the lively survival of historicist language in the period between the two world wars. Del Giudice, who developed an innovative design for the Stabilimento dei Bagni, or bath house, and other villas on the Lido, here uses the 1930s-baroque, at once free and rigorous, that so distinguishes his building style.

Casinò Municipale al Lido (Municipal Casino at the Lido)

Set on the Piazzale del Casinò is the geometric volume of the palazzo that houses the summer location of the Municipal Casino. This is the site of the Batteria delle Quattro Fontane, one of the many lesser nineteenth-century fortifications built by the Venetian Republic to defend the littoral. The Casino was built between 1936 and 1938 in a sober monumental style clearly referring to examples of rationalist architecture. The building was designed by the architect Eugenio Miozzi—who also designed the Garage INA in Piazzale Roma as well as the Ponte degli Scalzi—a major figure in the modernization of Venice by the Fascist regime. Inside, the various rooms are marked by a decorative experimentation in which Murano glass and mosaics are combined with chrome and exquisite marble.

Olivetti Retail Outlet

On the north side of Piazza San Marco stands the sixteenth-century Procuratie Vecchie, headquarters—until the fall of the Venetian Republic—of the highest magistracies of the city. The ground floor is punctuated by fifty archways intended for use as shops, and snugly housed here is the Olivetti retail outlet, praised by many critics as a masterpiece of modern architecture. Built in 1957 at the orders of Adriano Olivetti (a remarkable individual and one of the most enthusiastic supporters of the development of new forms of expression in the dynamic Italian postwar culture) the store was designed Carlo Scarpa, the late, noted contemporary architect, and the architectural bard of modern Venice. The harmonious spatial configuration of the store, at once lively and poised, is distinguished by a concerted interaction of diverse materials, which in the final analysis are the stars of Scarpa's work. The exquisite simplicity of the stone staircase is juxtaposed with the rough surface of the reinforced concrete, and the brilliant smooth stucco, contained and enlivened by wooden moldings. Of the same stone as the staircase, the geometric slab from which an incredibly fine sheet of water pours uninterruptedly is at once a Zen metaphor and a leitmotiv throughout Scarpa's entire body of work. The flooring in tiles of Murano glass in four different colors is an attempt to recreate the optical effects of a purely Venetian phenemenon to which this store and most of Venice is frequently subjected—flooding.

Fondazione Querini Stampalia

Proscribed for their role in the unsuccessful coup attempt by Bajamonte Tiepolo in 1310, a number of members of the Querini family took asylum in Stampalia (Astipalea), a Greek island that they owned, and which became part of the family name. Probably on the occasion of the wedding of Francesco Querini to Paola Priuli in 1528, this branch of the Querini family built this sober Renaissance palazzo. It was Giovanni Querini, the last scion of the family, who bequeathed to the city his vast collection of books, his own art collection, and the lavish eighteenth- and nineteenth-century furnishings that fill the halls and rooms, with their exquisite stuccoes, in a precocious neoclassical style. Now there are seven hundred paintings in the collection, including renowned canvases by Pietro Longhi and Gabriel Bella, while the library contains over three hundred thousand books, periodicals, and rare manuscripts, making the foundation one of the most dynamic cultural centers in the city.

Between 1961 and 1963 the ground floor of the palazzo was completely rebuilt by Carlo Scarpa, who also redesigned the garden, rife with Zen touches. The project included a display room and an atrium paved with marble tiles in three different colors. A walkway sheltered by the concrete and stone embankment runs along the water, which is channeled so that it flows freely through the buildings. An interplay of volumes in concrete animates the central section, filtered only by the gates that close off the arches of the portico. The interweaving of the brickwork, the subtle line of gold that marks the stone facings, the sophisticated chromatic composition—all are elements of Scarpa's poetics, a brilliant aesthetic universe filled with signs and styles taken from the local architectural tradition and from his Japanese inspirations.

Casa Gardella

This building is perhaps the best-known example of modern architecture set in the historical city of Venice. The architect Ignazio Gardella was opposed to an anti-historical reutilization of the past, and in 1954 planned a high-impact structure with little in common with the surrounding buildings. During the four years of construction, however, Gardella progressively abandoned his rigorous stance, and the design was modified to become a link between modernity and tradition. The smooth surface of the socle, reminiscent of the ground-floor rustication of many Venetian palazzi, is perforated by three sets of rhomboid apertures. The balcony on the second floor disappears and the volumes shrink as the gaze rises, while the windows multiply, in a playful inversion of solids and voids in the Gothic residential style of architecture. The terrace atop the building and the materials ranging from the ground earthenware in the plaster to the biancone di Vicenza for the socle are yet further citations in keeping with the Venetian tradition of building.

308

Residential Complex of the IACP at the Giudecca

Behind the Mulino Stucky extends a quarter designed by Gino Valle in 1980 to revive an often-overlooked and marginal area. In keeping with the industrial architecture present throughout the Giudecca and the models of "lesser" architecture represented there, Valle conceived of a gridwork of narrow compact modules organized in transverse bands. A network of paths and shared spaces extends within this residential grid, which has a strongly accented "familiar," and a powerfully Venetian nature.

Residential Complex of Sacca Fisola

As a completion of the urban conversion of Sacca Fisola, between 1982 and 1989 two separate complexes of public housing were built, each of them organized around a square courtyard.

Water, the element that clearly characterizes the city of Venice, runs freely among the piers (reminiscent of the original local Gothic architecture) that support the building, forming aquatic garages for mooring and maintenance of private vessels. Further evidence of the local architectural style can be found in the stone fascias of the horizontal courses which stand out against the colorful facades, while the continual windows are clearly inspired by those of Baldassarre Longhena. The complex was designed and built by the architects Iginio Cappai, Pietro Mainardis, and Valeriano Pastor.

Residential Complex of the Area Ex-Saffa

This residential complex, built between 1981 and 1989 by Vittorio Gregotti with the assistance of several other architects, was meant as a way of stitching back together the urban spaces and paths of the quarter of San Giobbe. The new work, distinguished by exceedingly simple facades in which only the roof balconies seek out a link with the local tradition, was sharply differentiated from the existing buildings in the area. Emphasized architectural elements constitute the focal points of the shared community space.

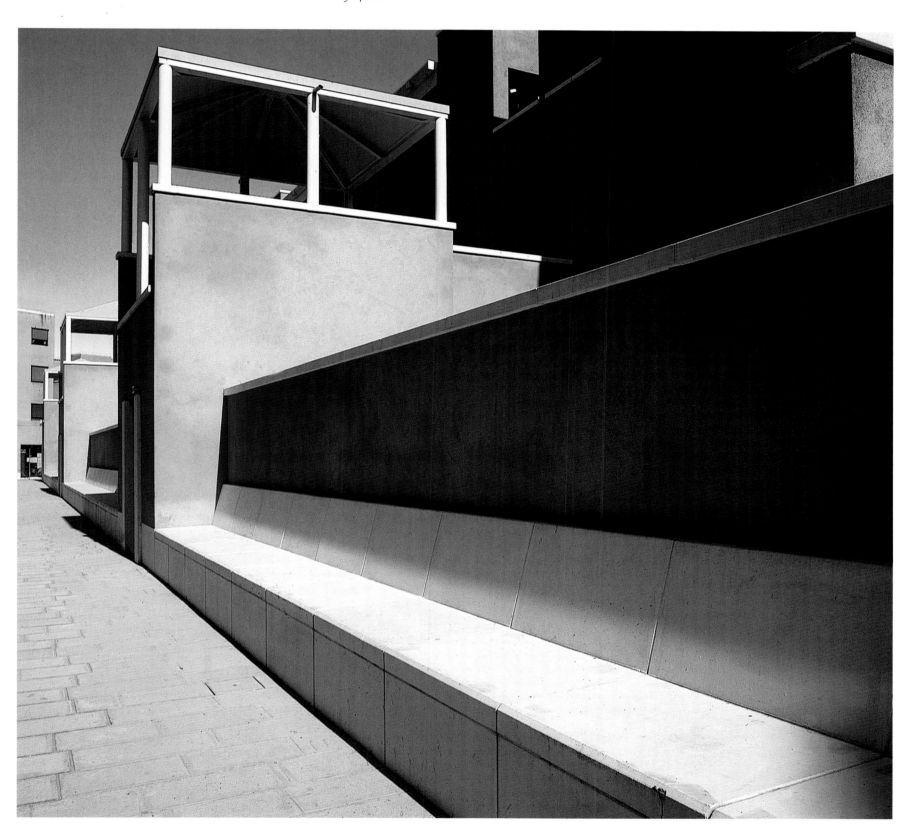

Designed for the aristocratic Venier family by Lorenzo Boschetti in 1749, this palazzo remained unfinished after the ground floor with its massive rustication had been completed. Now it is the site of the Museo Guggenheim, in which, beginning in 1942, Peggy Guggenheim assembled a collection of modern and contemporary art. In the courtyard of the building, which overlooks the Grand Canal, stands the Angel of the Citadel by Marino Marini, an isolated, enigmatic bronze dating from 1948. On a pedestal framed by a window is the Maiastra by Costantin Brancusi, a bronze dating from 1912. The halls of the palazzo, which are arranged now in accordance with the demands of exhibition spaces, were until recently quite simply the residence of the American arts patron and collector. The masterpiece of the building was her bedroom, dominated by the headboard designed and built by Alexander Calder. The collection is truly remarkable, including work by Picasso, Giacometti, Arp, Braque, Duchamp, Gris, Delaunay, Archipenko, and Lipchitz, displayed alongside paintings by Pollock and the surrealist artist Max Ernst, who was married to Peggy Guggenheim. This remarkable patron of the arts not only supported artists, but also served as a link between the various great avant-garde schools, especially those in the Americas, and the new Italian avant-garde. From Emilio Vedova and Afro (Basaldella), to Tancredi, Piero Dorazio, Edmondo Bacci, and Armando Pizzinato, the collection of paintings offers a major cross-section of Italian contemporary art from the Second World War to the present day.

Museo Archeologico (Archeological Museum)

From the portico of the Libreria Marciana, across the notably vertical courtyard by Vincenzo Scamozzi, one enters the halls of the museum. The collection includes Greek sculpture, architectural fragments, statues (including the renowned Dying Galatian, below), Roman epigraphs, as well as a collection of Roman coins, with items dating back to the third-to-first centuries B.C. This museum also houses the archeological section of the Museo Correr. The first nucleus of this museum was formed as early as 1523 when Domenico Cardina Grimani bequeathed to the Venetian Republic his renowned breviary, as well as Roman marble and bronze statues, which were at first put on display in a hall of Palazzo Ducale. Added to these sculptures were those bequeathed in 1587 by the cardinal's nephew Giovanni Grimani, Patriarch of Aquileia—these include a number of Greek statues. In 1597 Scamozzi was commissioned to renovate the vestibule of the Libreria Marciana in order to accommodate the by-then considerable collection, which had grown by various patrician bequests; most notable of these were from the Contarini and Nani families, and the possessions of the suppressed Paduan monastery of San Giovanni di Verdara. The collection was moved back to Palazzo Ducale after the fall of the Serenissima in 1812, and in 1924 after various wanderings the collection found its present-day location on a floor of the Procuratie Nuove.

Suggestions for further reading

Ackerman, James S. *Palladio*. Viking Penguin, 1974 (rev. edition).

Blunt, A. *Artistic Theory in Italy 1450–1600*. London, 1940.

Boito, Camilo, ed. *The Basilica of St. Mark in Venice Illustrated from the Points of View of Art and History by Venetian Writers*. Translated by William Scott. Gordon Press, 1976.

Constant, Caroline. *The Palladio Guide*. Princeton Architecture, 1993.

Cosgrove, Denis. *The Palladian Landscape: Geographical Change & Its Cultural Representations in Sixteenth-Century Italy*. Pennsylvania State University Press, 1993.

Demus, O. *The Church of San Marco in Venice*. Washington, D.C., 1960.

Farber, Joseph and Henry H. Reed. *Palladio's Architecture and Its Influences: A Photographic Guide*. Dover, 1980.

Goy, Richard. *Buildings of Venice*. Chronicle Books, 1994.

Goy, Richard. *The House of Gold: Building a Palace in Medieval Venice*. Cambridge University Press, 1993.

Haskell, F. *Patrons and Painters: A Study in the Relations Between Italian Art and Society in the Age of the Baroque*. New Haven and London, 1966–1985 (2nd edition).

Howard, D. *Jacopo Sansovino: Architecture and Patronage in Renaissance Venice*. New Haven and London, 1975.

Howard, D. *The Architectural History of Venice*. London, 1980.

Lorenzetti, G. *Venice and its Lagoon*. Trieste, 1994 (1st edition 1926).

Rogers, Elizabeth F. *Peter Lombard and the Sacramental System*. Richwood Publishers, 1976.

Ruskin, J. *The Stones of Venice*. Orpington, 1866.

Schulz, J. *The Printed Plans and Panoramic Views of Venice (1479–1797)*. Firenze, 1970.

Tavernor, Robert. *Palladio and Palladianism*. Thames and Hudson, 1991.

Wittkower, R. *Art and Architecture in Italy 1600 to 1750*. London, 1958.

Map

The numbers following the place name refer to the page of the text description. Buildings that do not appear on the map are marked "off map".

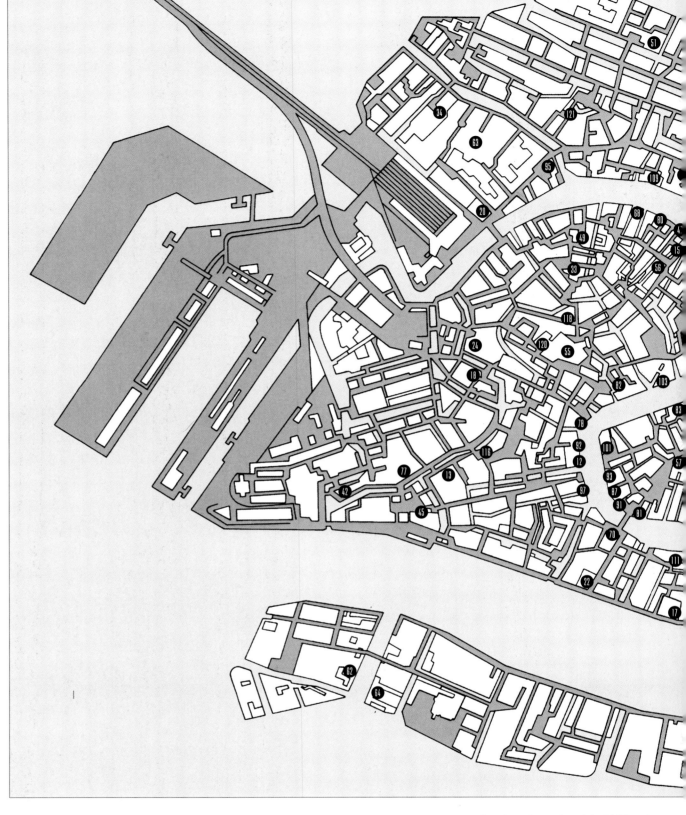

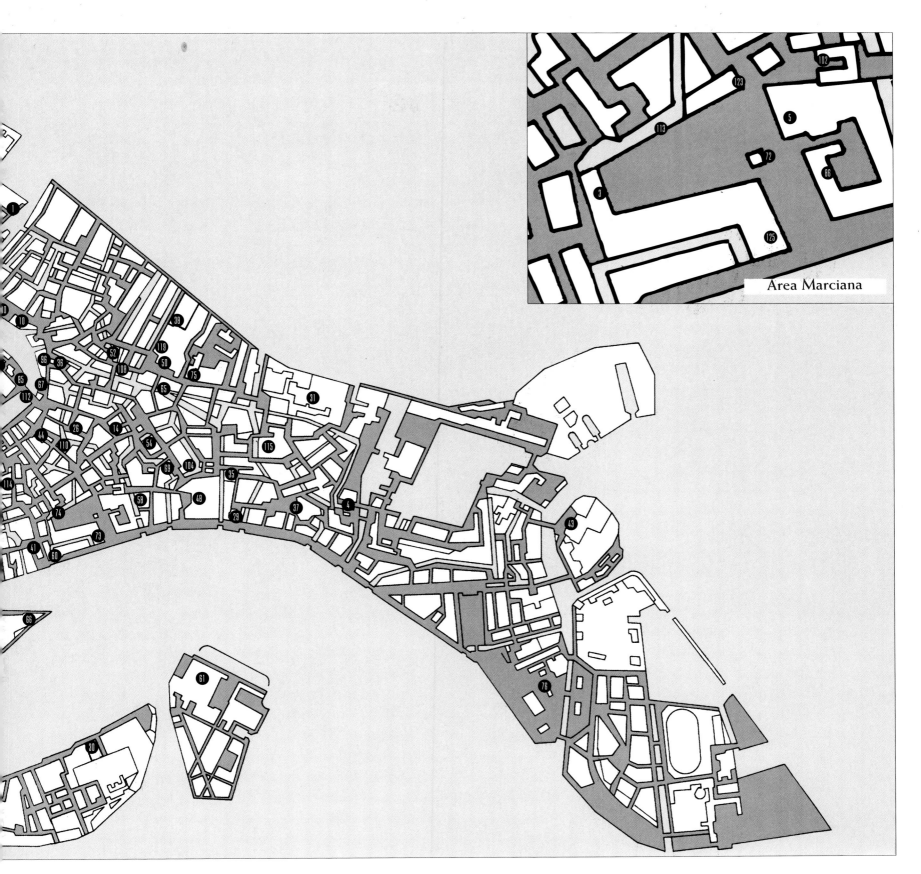

Area Marciana